HOMES & COURTYARDS

28 Beautifully Designed Homes For Outdoor Living

HOMES & COURTYARDS

28 Beautifully Designed Homes For Outdoor Living

BASSENIAN / LAGONI ARCHITECTS

A Book By Bassenian/Lagoni Architects
Copyright © 2007 by Bassenian/Lagoni Architects
Copyright © 2017 by Bassenian/Lagoni Architects

Library of Congress Control Number:
2007924321

International Standard Book Number:
ISBN-13: 978-0-9721539-3-5 (hardcover)
ISBN-10: 0-9721539-3-4 (hardcover)
ISBN-13: 978-0-9721539-8-0 (softcover)
ISBN-10: 0-9721539-8-5 (softcover)

Published by Bassenian/Lagoni Architects
2031 Orchard Drive, Suite 100
Newport Beach, CA 92660-0753
Phone: 949-553-9100
Fax: 949-553-0548
www.bassenianlagoni.com

Corporate
Chairman & CEO: Aram Bassenian, AIA
President: Carl Lagoni, AIA
Executive Vice President: Jeffrey LaFetra, AIA
Chief Financial Officer: Lee Rogaliner
Senior Principals: Scott Adams, AICP
                David Kosco, AIA
                Jeff Lake, AIA
Principals: Ali Badie, AIA
                Steven Dewan, AIA
                Ken Niemerski, AIA

Book Production
Editorial Director: Aram Bassenian, AIA
Editor-in-Chief: Rickard Bailey, Bailey Consulting, Inc.
Editor: Heather McCune
Writer: Laura Hurst Brown, Rascal Words, Ltd.
Design/Art Director: Edie Motoyama
Art Director/Designer, Cover Design: Zareh Marzbetuny, ZM Design
Floor Plan Graphics: Stacie Arrigo, Jennifer Cram, Edie Motoyama
Assistants to the Editorial Director: Kele Dooley, Debby Owens

Prepress by Toppan Hong Kong

Printed in China by Toppan Printing

10 9 8 7 6 5 4 3 2

Contents

Acknowledgements

BY ARAM BASSENIAN, AIA

Publishing has taken us on a rapid and eventful journey. It has been only two years since the publication of our second book, *Tuscan and Andalusian Reflections*, and just four years since we published our first volume, *Pure California*. Now, in *Homes and Courtyards*, we present our most extensive architectural work to date, with many of the homes emphasizing outdoor living. Such design evolution is our response to the changing needs of a robust economy in the United States and in emerging economies worldwide. There seems to be a clear recognition that home ownership is a substantial economic pillar in any growing society. To this we attribute a part of our success and for this we are thankful.

At Bassenian/Lagoni Architects, we cultivate a problem-solving and practical design attitude. Our company culture dictates that constraints are mere opportunities to be exploited for new and dynamic architecture. We firmly believe that our role is to assist the development team; thus, to us, excellence in service is a daily mantra. Therefore, we express our deep appreciation to a very unique team of talented professionals who constitute our firm. It is only the very passionate and mature design professional who has the ability to step up, time and time again, to offer fresh and diverse solutions— and we salute those in our office who do just that on a daily basis.

We are indebted as well to many of our clients, both builder and marketing executives, whose vision begins the design process for these beautiful homes and communities. They are courageous "place-makers" in the full sense of the definition. And our gratitude extends to their project managers and construction teams who embrace this vision and, through commitment and hard work, complete the mission with excellence.

We also extend sincere appreciation to our allied professionals—the structural engineers, landscape architects and interior designers who help make every new home an unfolding chapter in the American dream. It is only through total commitment to their craft that sticks and stones turn to comfort and elegance.

Lastly and importantly, I am forever indebted to my enlightened parents who willingly, and at a late age, sacrificed all to bring their children to this "shining city on the hill." Along the way they demonstrated the virtues of work, yet taught me moderation and balance in all matters of life. I am so grateful to America for affording me and my family education and, therefore, endless opportunity. And, closest to home, my deepest appreciation goes to my family for giving my life true purpose, guidance and stability.

Foreword

RIGHT PLACES

BY SANDRA KULLI, MIRM

This is what I prayed for ... a piece of land — not so very big, with a garden and, near the house, a spring that never fails, and a bit of wood to round it off.

— Horace

Now, more than 20 centuries later, we live at a pace Horace could not have imagined in 30 B.C. In our 24/7 world, with more gadgets, Google Earth, ways to design a car or plan a vacation on-line, we multi-task to manage work, family, pets, aging parents, what to eat for dinner, and, of course, e-mail. But much like Horace, we dream about a home, *our* home on our land, a place of beauty, respite, warmth, at one with nature, a place that's right for us.

Bassenian/Lagoni Architects' magic is in creating right places. Their homes give us refuge from the hectic world and shelter in its deepest, best meaning. They ground us in the land, the courtyard gardens, the beautiful interior spaces and the diverse exteriors that enrich the neighborhoods where they are built.

Frederic March, in his book, *Thunder at Twilight*, noted that all great places have two things in common: one foot in memory and one foot in prophecy. Bassenian/Lagoni imbues their architecture with that truth — creating homes that embody the best traditions of design — through materials, proportions and architectural styles. At the same time, their work embraces and celebrates the future with clean lines, simple elegance and artful form, bringing the art in architecture to every home.

In traveling the globe, from Tuscan Italy to Moorish Spain, and from the New England coast to the American Southwest, Bassenian/Lagoni designers have tapped into the world-influences on great architecture. And they've drawn on the best of America's rich residential heritage. From Neff to Maybeck and from Gill to Wright, their work weaves together memory and prophecy.

The noted mid-century California architect, Cliff May, once designed a two-room house with a five-room garden. The courtyard homes displayed in this volume honor the notion of that connectivity. Natural light seems to penetrate each of these homes so seamlessly. Whether it is an expansive veranda or a central courtyard, the outdoors consistently activates the core and elements of each of these houses with inventiveness. Outdoor living truly has an allure all of its own and these wondrous homes blend the dreams of the owner and architect with the land and garden. Bassenian/Lagoni's work accentuates that combination in its creative best—*right places*.

As a child, I grew up on Prospect Boulevard in Pasadena — one of the streets mentioned in Allan Jacobs' *Great Streets* classic. From the camphor-tree canopy to the Wallace Neff, Greene and Greene, and Frank Lloyd Wright homes, my neighborhood was filled with architectural gems and landscape grandeur. As a youngster, I took it for granted that all neighborhoods were this wonderful. It spoiled me for the future – and made other right places so much more valuable when I found them.

In the pages of this book, you'll see homes that are distinctive and that resonate with the feeling of *right place* for the right homeowner. Therein lies the practical genius of Bassenian/Lagoni Architects' work. Whether designing a one-family custom home, like the Wine Country Residence in Paso Robles, or a whole development neighborhood, like Bella Fioré in Lake Las Vegas, Bassenian/Lagoni Architects create homes as different and distinctive as their owners, things of beauty with extraordinary character and appeal...*right places*. And like the great neighborhoods of the past, I long to live in one. That's their magic.

Introduction

TRADITION AND INNOVATION

BY ARAM BASSENIAN, AIA & CARL LAGONI, AIA

Tradition and innovation — two seemingly contradictory influences — often contribute equally to the architecture that shapes our lives. Consider the following definitions:

Tradition: an inherited, established customary pattern of thought, action or behavior; the handing down of information, beliefs, and customs from one generation to another without written instruction.

Innovation: the introduction of something new; to effect a change in something.

Architecture consistently draws inspiration from the past and modifies the original to express a new aesthetic that reflects current ways of thinking. Historical influences for our work have come from masters such as:

Andrea Palladio, one of the most influential architects in the Western world, was prolific in Northern Italy during the sixteenth century. Drawing great inspiration from classical architecture, he generated a carefully proportioned vocabulary that became the model for stately homes and government buildings in both Europe and in America.

Wallace Neff was instrumental in his impact on Southern California's early residential architecture. Reflecting the Moorish idioms of the Mediterranean climate zone, his homes designed for movie moguls appeared in the 1930s. Today, they are the epitome of that era with an eloquence untainted by the passage of time.

To architect *Charles Moore* we credit the ignition of the more playful Post-Modern movement. The significance of his contribution is immeasurable. Through him, in part, modernism was rapidly transformed, allowing architects freedom for open experimentation.

Ricardo Legorreta, a noted designer from Mexico, has authored an architectural language that combines bold, clean, colorful forms with the character of the Southwest. His work stands out for its simplicity and sculptural singularity.

These masters create designs so substantive that they seem to transcend time and place. As architects who follow, our role is to understand the essence of their work and, using today's technology and building materials, create up-to-date homes reflective of contemporary lifestyle.

Today, as a firm, we find ourselves practicing during a unique time in history. Buoyed by an expanding economy, we have multiple opportunities for creativity. At the same time, our design efforts are occurring in a highly competitive marketplace. This milieu fuels advancement and evolution — motivating us to continuously reach for the next and more sophisticated home. And through our involvement with development housing, we are gratified to touch so many in America as they pursue their home-ownership dream.

In the following pages we unveil homes that represent our current contribution to the evolving art form that is housing. With ordered architecture, fractured massing and brick and stone detailing, we recall the hill towns of Tuscany at *Castellina*. The interiors of these upscale townhomes are designed to naturally flow out to balconies, loggias and extended patios to enthusiastically connect with the soft climate of coastal Southern California.

At the *Shady Canyon Residence*, a layering of spaces is unveiled through controlled openings. A progression unfolds to reveal the spatial experiences of this unique home. Formal and informal as well as indoor and outdoor living areas are contained with unity in a rural Mediterranean theme.

The *Wine Country Residence* in Paso Robles rests on a spectacular hilltop. Combine this great site with the ideal client and you have the once-in-a-lifetime opportunity for any architectural firm. Here with crisp, contemporary lines and inspiration from Legorreta, the front and back of this dwelling open to meet the vineyards of central California.

And it all comes together at *The Tides* in Newport Coast. Residential architecture, with inspiration from Tuscany, turns to express a new aesthetic in upscale coastal living. An entry forecourt, followed by a three-story interior courtyard, is enhanced by exquisite brick and stone detailing, bringing the outdoors inside and stimulating our senses.

As you experience this photographic home tour with its attendant narrative, we hope you find in our homes and communities a respect for tradition with a flare that speaks of innovation.

CHAPTER ONE

HOMES & COURTYARDS

The Tides

BUILDER: STANDARD PACIFIC HOMES • LOCATION: NEWPORT COAST, CALIFORNIA • PHOTOGRAPHY: ANTHONY GOMEZ

RESIDENCE ONE

Perched above a breathtaking stretch of the Pacific coastline, this richly detailed Mediterranean home captures the strong lines of a classic Tuscan farmhouse. Just beyond the formal entry forecourt, the house reveals its dramatic surprise: a stunning three-story second courtyard that allows sunlight and coastal breezes to penetrate and infuse the center of this magnificent home. As the sequence of spaces unfolds, the building takes shape with well-delineated mixes of stone and stucco that visually connect the house with the coastal grandeur of the site. Vistas extend beyond the rear loggia and terrace to the horizon, where glimpses of the sea confer a sense of tranquility on the home. Public rooms on the main and lower levels relate closely to the subterranean garden, a refreshing counterpoint to the rustic sophistication of the interior. Open to the sky, the courtyards complement exposure to the outdoors at the front and rear of the home, and lend light and protection from the elements at its core.

Right | Worthy of its upscale location, the house achieves visual continuity with the site and opens to an uninterrupted vista that extends from the sidewalk to the sea. Despite its apparent size and grandeur, the home contains an elegant floor plan that lives principally on one level.

Below | Centuries collide at the rear perimeter, where detailed brick surrounds, stone cladding and a trio of arches play against the clean lines of a very up-to-date home. A ribbon of vertical windows flanking the upper loggia captures vast views of the sea.

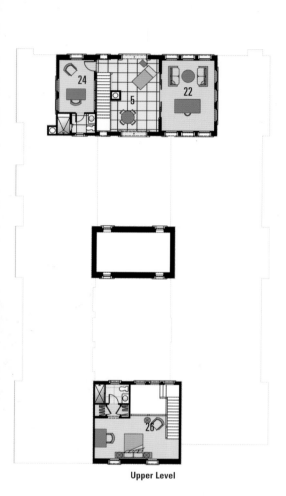

Upper Level

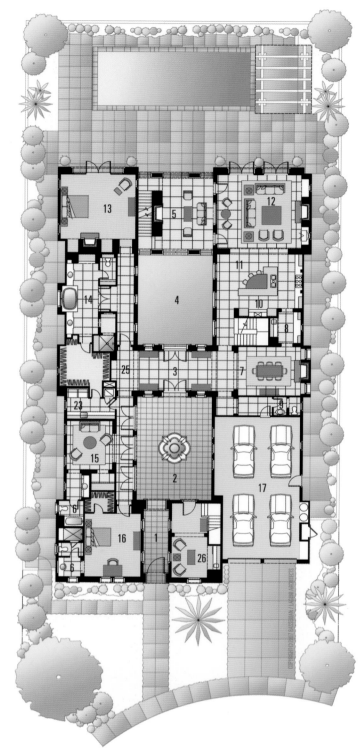

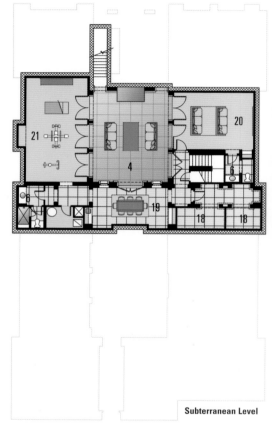

Subterranean Level

Legend

1 Breezeway	10 Kitchen	19 Wine Tasting Room
2 Forecourt	11 Nook	20 Home Theater
3 Foyer	12 Family Room	21 Fitness Room
4 Central Courtyard	13 Master Bedroom	22 Artist Loft
5 Loggia	14 Master Bathroom	23 Laundry
6 Bathroom	15 Den	24 Office
7 Dining Room	16 Bedroom Suite	25 Gallery Hall
8 Butler's Pantry	17 Garage	26 Casita
9 Powder Room	18 Wine Cellar	

7,171 SQUARE FEET

About The Floor Plan: Influenced by rural Mediterranean antecedants, the plan is defined by groups of simple, rectilinear shapes. Oriented toward the sea, the house opens at the entry foyer to a finely crafted central courtyard, offering an unexpected view of the whole house. With livability focused on the main floor, the home is enhanced with a two-story casita at the entry, an artist loft and office on the upper floor, and a fitness room, wine cellar and home theater below.

Opposite Page | Hand-applied plaster finishes, exposed rafter tails and flourishes of wrought iron reference elements of rural Italian villas at the courtyard. An open foyer overlooks the central courtyard, which functions as an outdoor living area, linked to a wine cellar and wine tasting room via French doors.

Opposite Page Above | An intimately scaled foyer intersects the plan at the entry, creating a spatial connection between the forecourt and the central courtyard, and linking the formal and private wings of the home.

Opposite Page Below | A fusion of coastal influences creates a striking balance of clean, cosmopolitan lines and rural character in the formal dining room. The muted palette of sand-pebble hues provides an ideal canvas for the space's more striking furnishings.

Above | Rough stone walls and a timber ceiling alter the depth and dimension of the informal living area viewed from the open kitchen. A scalloped, square arch adds subtle definition to the space, accentuated by a shift to hardwood from travertine floors.

Above | Open to views of the ocean, the master bedroom offers a seamless boundary to the rear terrace, pool and deck. The deep, umber tones of the hardwood floor are contradicted by the sleek lines of a marble fireplace surround.

Below Left | The vintage garden tub sets the tone in the master bath, which offers splendid amenities, such as a walk-through closet, separate lavs and vanities, and a step-in dual shower.

Above | Sliding French doors open the upper-level artist's loft to the upper loggia, where wide views of the horizon are absorbed by the interior. Three windows—like ship's portals—bring in natural light and long thoughts of the sea.

Below Right | Timber trusses and a flagstone deck add dimension and color to a partially enclosed sitting area at the upper loggia. Ocean breezes flow through the space even when the drapes are closed.

Opposite Page | The purity of the design stems from the symmetry that is evident at the central courtyard—a playful, unexpected element that brings light into the core of the home. Varied textures of wood, stone, timber and brick soften the scale of the home, and call up ageless traditions that add depth to its character.

Right | French doors open the house to the amenities of the back property, a fitting environment for owners who love the outdoors. A blend of natural materials—clay roof tiles and timber beams—authenticate the elevation's rural theme.

Above | Located near the top of a hillside, the waters of a lap pool appear to rise to the level of the sea. An extensive terrace provides unobstructed views for lounging sunbathers.

Below | At the edge of the rear property, a pergola shelters an outdoor eating area, adjacent to an alfresco kitchen packed with luxe amenities such as dual commercial-grade grills.

Above | At the rear elevation, a simple stone-clad central mass is flanked by single-story stucco structures, evoking the scale of early Tuscan homes. A covered staircase connects the levels of a two-story loggia that increases light and circulation throughout the plan.

Bella Fioré
at Lake Las Vegas

BUILDER: PARDEE HOMES • LOCATION: HENDERSON, NEVADA
PHOTOGRAPHY: ERIC FIGGE

THE COMMUNITY

Set against the wide-open scenery of the high desert, this community of courtyard homes overlooks the jagged outcroppings of hillsides surrounding an area well within view of the famed Las Vegas Strip. Influenced by Andalusian, Tuscan and Italian Renaissance design themes, the houses employ cultured stone and barrel tile to create harmonious links to the environment. A stone's throw from the amenities of Lake Las Vegas Resort, the neighborhood is a natural extension of the waterfront community, with a precisely orchestrated look that pairs recessed entries, forecourts and courtyards with the varied rooflines of a village environment. One- and two-story elevations engage well-scaled proportions and traditional details—bracketed cornices, classic brick arches, overhanging eaves and sculpted columns—to underscore their link to the past, yet the homes are flexible, highly functional and environmentally friendly. Walls of glass convey a pleasing sense of space inside, integrating wide panels of scenery with rooms that also provide a sense of protection and shelter.

Above | Elemental materials, varied rooflines and broken massing create a gracious, human-scaled elevation, invigorated by textured planes, deeply recessed windows and a bold tower that harbors the entry.

Opposite Page Above | Granite-slab countertops and maple cabinetry complement sleek stainless-steel appliances in a gourmet kitchen designed for two cooks. A sculpted passageway leads to the formal dining room through a well-equipped butler's pantry.

Opposite Page Center | An open arrangement of the family room, morning nook and kitchen creates interplay between the cool polished tones of the food-preparation area and the cultivated look of the rear garden.

Opposite Page Below | Views extend beyond the rear perimeter to a spacious yard that repeats the pure, linear dimensions of the house. A covered loggia unites the master wing with an informal eating area, exemplifying the home's indoor-outdoor aesthetic.

Opposite Page Above | Amenities in the spa-like master bath include a step-in dual shower, a garden tub and a well-organized walk-in closet. A leaded-glass window and a recessed vanity affirm the lush character of the owners' retreat.

Opposite Page Center | In the gourmet kitchen, paneled cabinetry and a midnight-black tiled backsplash contribute to the European feel of the home. A crescent-shaped island orients the work spaces toward the morning room and overlooks the back property.

Above | Pure-white brackets and overhanging eaves play counterpoint to a barrel-tile roof and Venetian-red plaster on an elaborate façade derived from the villas of Italy. The forecourt leads to a foyer and an inviting transition to the formal living spaces.

Opposite Page Below | Stepped massing at the rear elevation creates separation of the outside spaces, which include a quiet courtyard accessed from the living room. Transom windows accentuate the curved wall of glass that brightens the vaulted family room.

Shady Canyon Residence

LOCATION: IRVINE, CALIFORNIA • PHOTOGRAPHY: ERIC FIGGE

Within a master-planned community fringed by a nature preserve and surrounded by coastal wilderness, the rubble-stone elevation of this custom courtyard home captures the spirit of a rugged Tuscan farmhouse. At the front of the plan, a 1½-story presentation conveys the simplicity of a rural villa and assigns a human scale to the streetscene. An understated forecourt allows glimpses of the central courtyard from the outside, and adds depth and dimension to a processional approach to the formal entry. Anchored by a central turret, the two-story rear elevation frames the central courtyard, which activates the primary living areas, infusing the rooms with natural light. Defined by a series of open spaces, the courtyard is enhanced with pavers and small gardens, and fused by a palette of natural materials. Inside, half-walls and flagstone steps combine with stairs and arches to define the multiple levels. At the upper courtyard, the steel-and-glass doors of a home office open on a graveled path that crosses to a covered court. Four steps lead to a lower-level fountain court that visually extends the casual living areas. Rooms on the upper floor benefit from the union of light and air brought in by a Juliet balcony overlooking the outdoor arena.

About The Floor Plan: A rectangular footprint encircles a courtyard that penetrates the plan on two levels, unified by a textured elevation of brick, stone and stucco. Single-level wings to the front of the plan provide both public and private spaces: a home office, guest quarters and a game room. To the rear of the plan, first-floor rooms radiate from a rotunda and stairwell, and lead to an open arrangement in the informal zone.

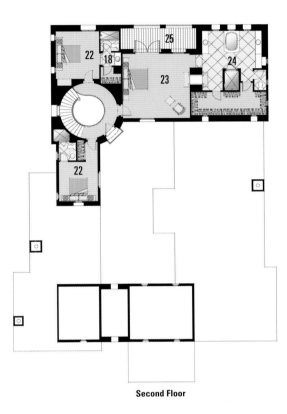

Second Floor

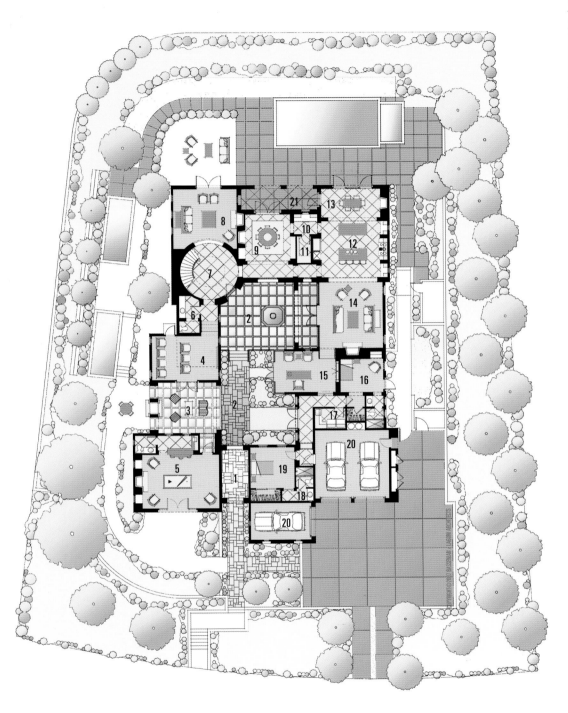

Opposite Page Above | Two distinct ceiling treatments permit a varied approach to the design scheme. In the family room, umber-hued beams offer contrast to the crème-colored ceiling.

Opposite Page Below | The linear proportions of the kitchen and morning nook are offset by rugged timbers and a plank ceiling above a wall of golden fieldstone. An arch of stacked brick articulates the boundary between the serving and eating areas.

Previous Page | Brick, stone, wood and iron dominate the public view of the central courtyard. Sequestered by a massive entry door, a narrow forecourt is framed by two rugged fieldstone piers and a brick arch.

Legend

1 Forecourt	8 Living Room	15 Home Office	22 Bedroom
2 Central Courtyard	9 Dining Room	16 Maid's Room	23 Master Bedroom
3 Covered Courtyard	10 Butler's Pantry	17 Laundry	24 Master Bathroom
4 Home Theater	11 Walk-in Pantry	18 Bathroom	25 Deck/Balcony
5 Game Room	12 Kitchen	19 Guest Bedroom	
6 Powder Room	13 Morning Room	20 Garage	
7 Entry Rotunda	14 Family Room	21 Loggia	

5,791 SQUARE FEET

Above | Playful lines at the entry artfully define the separation of the upper and lower floors. Corridor views extend the transitions to the living room and a gallery hall.

Right | The change in levels from the entry rotunda to the living room creates a purposeful division of space at the center of the home. An intimate grouping encircles the fireplace, which offsets the subdued spirit of the room with a commanding stone surround.

Above | Terracotta tile rooftops set among groves of cypress and olive trees bring to mind clusters of rural Italian houses perched on a scenic crest above the sea. The house is set in a community encompassing acres of canyons, hills and open spaces.

Opposite Page | A merger of house and garden occurs in the courtyard, where tile and stone create a unifying simplicity. French doors open the secluded home office to contemplative surroundings. Four steps down, an elegant stone fountain aligns with a set of glass doors leading to the family room.

Above | A covered side courtyard with an alfresco fireplace harbors an informal conversation group, adjacent to the home theater and a few steps from the game room. Heavy timber beams line the ceiling of this open-air room, designed to be simpatico with fieldstone walls and a floor of weathered-brick pavers.

Below | An olive tree casts shadows on the quiet side terrace and herb garden, where architectural forms of stone and tile step into the landscape. The through-fireplace is shared by the courtyard adjacent to the media room.

Above | Oriented toward the rear property, the upper-level master suite opens to a private deck with wide views of the preserved open spaces. Rough-hewn plank and beam ceilings contribute to the provincial charm of the owners' retreat, which provides a through-fireplace to the dual bath.

Below | Deep windows and recessed arches punctuate the two-story rear elevation. The simple rectangular massing is reminiscent of rural Mediterranean farmhouses. A covered loggia shelters an outdoor sitting area from the glare of the noonday sun.

Elements of
Design

Exterior Materials To The Inside

■ Eminently livable inside and out, this fresh interpretation of a rustic field-stone villa imparts a sense of the past to a comfortable home infused with a modern aesthetic. Tuned to the natural setting, the Tuscan-style plan introduces structural and design elements that create pleasing adjacencies with traditional materials. Rough-hewn corbels set off craggy stone piers and brick-laden arches in the courtyard, a theme that is repeated indoors with heavy timbers, ledgestone, tile and bricks. A steady play of natural materials throughout the interior erases the distinction between even the formal rooms and the outdoors. A purposeful confrontation of elements occurs at boundary transitions from the courtyard to refined areas of the home: the entry rotunda, for example, exhibits a vibrant mix of renaissance themes, with thick Roman arches, terracotta pavers, sculpted wrought-iron balusters and mosaic stair tiles. Sleek metal-and-glass doors affirm the contemporary nature of the home office and media room. Every corner of the home exhibits warmth and vitality made tangible by the presence of natural exterior materials. The primal qualities of each room reconcile a needed sense of safety and shelter with the innate pleasures of living outdoors.

Tremezzo at Lake Las Vegas

BUILDER: PARDEE HOMES • LOCATION: HENDERSON, NEVADA • PHOTOGRAPHY: ERIC FIGGE

RESIDENCE TWO

Overlooking Lake Las Vegas, this Mediterranean retreat encircles a central courtyard, open to the sky and wrapped by a tile-roofed colonnade. At the front of the home, a strong, weathered-brick turret harbors a vaulted portico that creates passage to the formal entrance through the forecourt. Asymmetrical rooflines establish a varied rhythm for the façade, so that the house appears to be formed by many buildings, simulating a hilltown structure. An L-shaped loggia, defined by spiral columns and wide, sculpted arches, lines the private core of the home and articulates the positive outside space. A gallery and open rooms are organized around the center court, amplifying circulation and increasing light throughout the plan. A spacious great room extends the ambience of the courtyard to the covered patio via double sets of French doors. Surrounded by fairways and within walking distance of Lake Las Vegas village, the master-down home offers a resort environment with plenty of room for friends and visitors. Interior living spaces offer site lines oriented toward wide views captured through walls of glass. The informality of the home is expressed by the order and versatility of the interior spaces: a family room or media center off the patio, a morning room adjoining the courtyard, a flexible, upper-level club room and a main-level home office that converts to a theater, den or fourth bedroom.

Legend

1 Entry Portal	7 Morning Room	13 Master Bedroom
2 Loggia	8 Laundry	14 Master Bathroom
3 Central Courtyard	9 Family Room	15 Bedroom
4 Living Room	10 Garage	16 Guest Suite
5 Dining Room	11 Gallery Hall	17 Home Theater
6 Kitchen	12 Powder Room	18 Club Room

3,726 SQUARE FEET

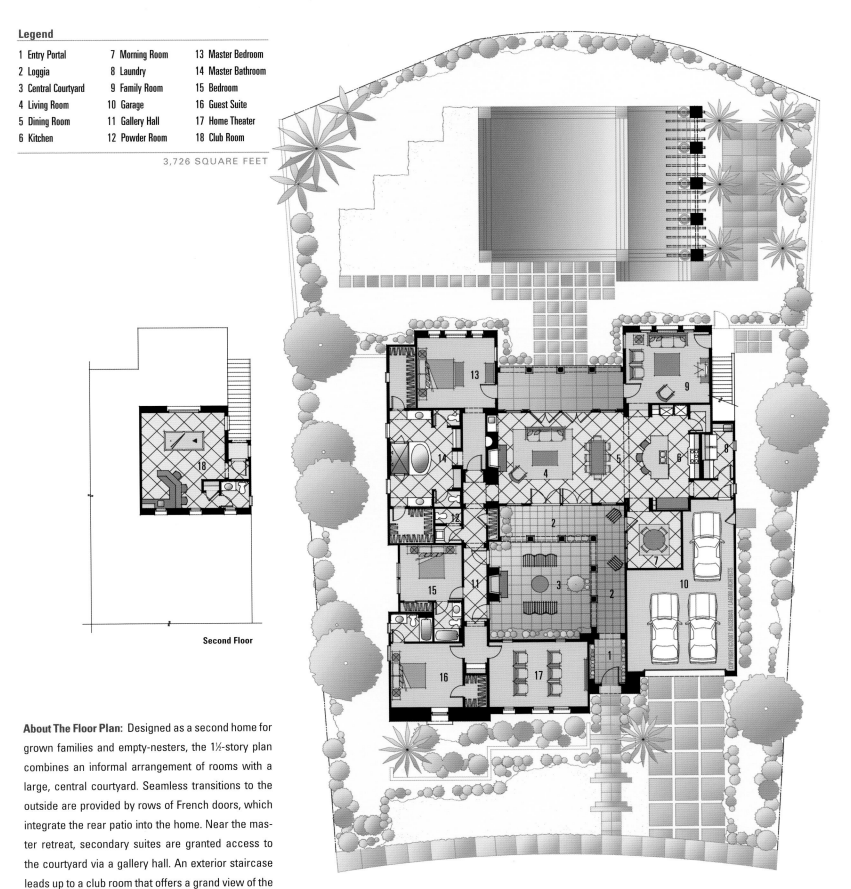

Second Floor

About The Floor Plan: Designed as a second home for grown families and empty-nesters, the 1½-story plan combines an informal arrangement of rooms with a large, central courtyard. Seamless transitions to the outside are provided by rows of French doors, which integrate the rear patio into the home. Near the master retreat, secondary suites are granted access to the courtyard via a gallery hall. An exterior staircase leads up to a club room that offers a grand view of the pool and spa and converts to guest quarters.

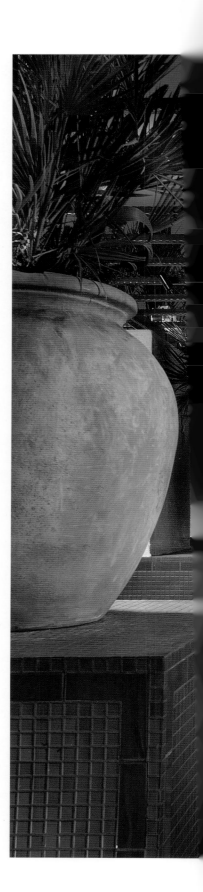

Above | Spiral columns and massive arches frame the center courtyard, anchored by an outdoor fireplace and wrapped with a loggia that shelters and subdues the space between the open-air living area and the house.

Right | Fractured massing at the rear elevation reveals Mediterranean instincts with a colonnade and a ribbon of clerestory windows. A shallow underwater deck permits the pool to lap the feet of a line of chaise lounges.

Casa Bonita del Rio

LOCATION: RANCHO SANTA FE, CALIFORNIA • PHOTOGRAPHY: ERIC FIGGE

Historic Rancho Santa Fe provides a perfect backdrop to the Early California theme of this one-of-a-kind home. Like an early-day *casa de pueblo*, a subdued entry framed by a vintage, Mission-style façade conceals a highly livable retreat of high-beamed ceilings, rustic stone arches and cool tiled floors. Mission influences inspired by the original masterworks of such regional luminaries as Wallace Neff and Lilian Rice translate easily to the open-air galleries of this single-level plan. Set on ten acres, the home fully engages its surroundings with outdoor entertainment areas, including a lush pool-and-spa environment and two loggias that ease the transitions from indoors to out. Sight lines extend the width of the house in two directions from the entry rotunda along the spine of the home, and offer engaging vistas of the back property. Flourishes of desert hues and rugged textures assign an authentic character to the home—a hacienda-style ranch house with strong ties to the outdoors. Vaulted arches add a wealth of character to individual rooms without detracting from the visual harmony and fluent dimensions that unite the home with its natural setting. Rows of windows bring in broad panels of scenery throughout the home, while along the rear perimeter, sliding glass walls achieve a seamless integration with the landscape.

Above | Heavy timber beams play harmony with a series of clerestory windows designed to offer privacy and glimpses of daylight. A brick archway frames a tranquil view of the front courtyard and fountain.

Previous Page | Varied rooflines accentuate the massing of the elevation, an asymmetrical arrangement of forms anchored by a central entry turret. A carved door opens to the *portal*, or entry hall, derived from Mission dialects.

Opposite Page | High-volume planked ceilings expand the vertical dimensions of the informal zone, a flexible entertainment area linked to the back property via a wide loggia. A raised-hearth fireplace with an intricately decorated tile surround offers a visual foil to the grand scale of the space.

Rimrock Summit

BUILDER: MASTERCRAFT HOMES
LOCATION: HIDDEN MEADOWS, CALIFORNIA • PHOTOGRAPHY: LANCE GORDON

THE COMMUNITY

This resort-style hilltop neighborhood caters to upscale professionals, employing a diverse architectural scheme, tailored amenities, flexible interiors and views that stretch westward to Catalina Island. Set in hilly terrain pocketed with boulders and swaths of chaparral, houses orient toward the distant sea, with outdoor retreats that overlook olive groves and other indigenous growth. Santa Barbara and Tuscan exterior styles with a menu of floor plans and options alter the look and function of individual homes, and create a custom-home feel throughout the community. The plans feature formal entries, stair halls and large public rooms, many of which capture the fifty-mile vista. Arched windows, precast-stone columns, brick turrets and hipped roofs contribute to design authenticity. Forecourts, porticos, casitas and sheltered porches reinforce the architectural expressions. Inside, open arrangements of the living and dining rooms, with vaulted foyers and balcony overlooks, complement impressive informal areas that connect easily with the outdoors. Versatile spaces—game rooms, dens, home offices and guest quarters—are marked by open archways and easy transitions that promote the function and flow of the homes.

Below | The open arrangement of the family room and kitchen, with a subtle sense of separation provided by a square arch, creates striking interior vistas. Paneled walls reference the kitchen's cherry-colored wood cabinetry and hardwood floors, visually uniting the area.

Opposite Page Top | A trio of clerestory glass panes allows glimpses of sky above a Palladian-style window that enriches the living room with views of the horizon. A sculpted arch opens the space to the formal dining room; the through-fireplace is shared with the adjacent den.

Opposite Page Center | The upper-level master suite provides a sitting area that opens to an expansive deck through a single French door. Light and views permitted by the large panel of windows enhance the connection to the outdoors.

Opposite Page Bottom | A series of arches creates a site line from the entry to the family room. Designed as a casual gathering space and command-central for traditional events, the kitchen offers flexible dining options.

Castellina at Covenant Hills

BUILDER: CENTEX HOMES • LOCATION: LADERA RANCH, CALIFORNIA • PHOTOGRAPHY: ERIC FIGGE

TOWNHOMES & FLATS

Stacked stone, terracotta tile and ochre-colored stucco call up the rugged, earthen forms of Italy's hill country in this prominent neighborhood of flats and townhomes. Streets follow the quiet contours of slopes and banks that wind through the community and conclude in idyllic destinations: circular piazzas wrapped by cul-de-sacs that layer even the primary traffic arteries with a sense of nature. Village trails link to parks and public spaces and maintain a friendly dialogue with the landscape. Tuscan-inspired exteriors reflect a spirited style yet express an affinity for the rural themes of the Italian originals. Multifaceted forms typify the low-pitched lines and fractured massing of the Mediterranean design, redefined as a diverse network of attached villas. Hipped and gabled rooftops and asymmetrical forms create a rhythm that tempers the scale of the structures and preserves a sense of intimacy. The imposing geometry is punctuated by rows of windows that open the homes to light and views. Covered loggias, verandas and decks invite the natural environment into the public and informal zones, and function well as outdoor rooms.

Previous Page | A playful informality prevails at the rear perimeter, where a series of courtyard-like settings enliven the balance of stucco, brick and wood. Fractured massing produces natural clusters of townhomes and flats, creating patterned angles of light that activate the individual units.

Opposite Page | Recessed double-sash windows set off a balance of stucco and stone on the exterior elevations, which swing side-loading garages away from the street thus reducing the dominance of the garage doors.

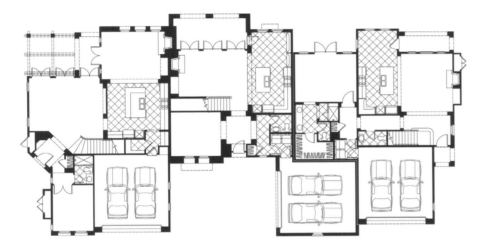

About The Floor Plan: Situated on an elevated site, the community contains 82 homes on approximately 11 acres, an arrangement that takes advantage of wonderful views. Organized into scaled neighborhoods by a spine street and its tributaries, the community also uses portal-type entry roads and sloped banks encircling land masses to further define its softscape boundaries. Two different building types offer varied elevations: two-story luxury plexes with individual covered loggias and verandas; and flats and multi-story units—such as a tri-level design with a loft retreat—linked to decks and verandas.

Above Left | The central element of this single-story floor plan is the formal dining room, a space that connects to the kitchen and living room, and leads outside to the covered loggia.

Left | An upper-level secondary bedroom enjoys plenty of light brought in by tall windows and a French door leading to a Juliet balcony. The suite provides a built-in planning desk, dual wardrobe and a private entertainment bar.

Below Left | This plan's simplicity is most evident in the living room, dining area and kitchen, where a square arch frames views and defines sight lines from one room to another.

Above | A broad square arch offers subtle definition to the family room and kitchen spaces at the front of this plan, expressing an airy aesthetic that is modern and cool. Hand-troweled ceilings, paneled beams and arches and cherry-stained floors create a pleasant ambiance.

Elements of
Design

Bringing The Outdoors In

Spacious patio areas in this award-winning townhome village accommodate outdoor rooms that significantly extend the livability of the interiors. The sloped site permits the building clusters to exploit valley views throughout the community, with floor plans oriented toward the rear perimeter. French doors take in the scenery and activate interior spaces with links to open-air verandas, patios and decks. Layered massing and asymmetrical forms permit daylight to enter the homes at oblique angles, creating interplay between the rear edges and streams of light. Rooms are allowed to dissolve into natural settings, infusing these reflections of old-world houses with a modern sense of space. Proportioned to accommodate conversation groups and informal meals, the outdoor rooms are furnishable in size and provide an airy place allied to indoor living areas. Timber beams and wood trellises offer a warm contrast to precast columns and stone floor tiles, contributing to the defining characteristics of the style. A series of brick-lined arches marks the rear perimeter of several plans, framing the views and creating a signature look to the rear elevation.

The Province

BUILDER: STANDARD PACIFIC HOMES • LOCATION: INDIAN WELLS, CALIFORNIA • PHOTOGRAPHY: ANTHONY GOMEZ

RESIDENCE FOUR

Classic architecture sets the tone for a desert community at Indian Wells. This Italianate villa reflects Old World traditions, with a recessed paneled entry harbored by a central turret that adds verticality to the single-story elevation. Bone-white plaster set off by wood-trim shutters and window elements hints at an early Mediterranean theme that is reinforced by cupola-like accents and a simple, clay-tiled roof. Airy colonnades and scores of windows open the home to wide views of the desert set against the profile of nearby Eisenhower Mountain. The formal plan progresses from the entry vestibule to a secluded living room, or parlor, through an extensive gallery that opens to the formal dining room and wraps the courtyard perimeter. Natural light brought in by a rear loggia is enhanced by spatial and visual connections to the side courtyard, which contains an inviting deck, pool and fountain. Throughout the home, sight lines draw guests into the public rooms, and help separate the entertainment areas from the quiet owners' retreat and private guest suites.

Above | Sculpted cornices and clay-tile roofs reveal the Mediterranean influences of this courtyard design. A decorative vent provides an idiomatic accent above a recessed entry and a series of unmatched windows.

Below | The side courtyard brings a sense of serenity that extends beyond the outdoor living area to the public and informal rooms, which wrap the outside space. Elements such as traditional coping of the pool and masonry pavers create an historic ambience.

Above | The gourmet kitchen boasts an island and serving counter that invites easy meals and family gatherings. Dark-stained floors and cabinets contrast with créme-colored walls and tile backsplash.

Below | A scalloped edge on the sculpted arch offers subtle definition to the space between the family room and kitchen. Carved details set apart the open arrangements of rooms throughout the home, providing separation without interfering with views.

Above | Double French doors open an airy master retreat to a private patio and spacious back property, engaging the warm, neutral tones of the interior with great outdoor vistas. Twin windows bring in glimpses of scenery and plenty of natural light.

The Province

BUILDER: STANDARD PACIFIC HOMES • LOCATION: INDIAN WELLS, CALIFORNIA • PHOTOGRAPHY: ANTHONY GOMEZ

RESIDENCE FIVE

In an established enclave of single-level residences, the home achieves a resort-style presence, with airy, informal living spaces connected to highly functional outdoor areas. At the street, layered massing shapes an asymmetrical arrangement of the central turret framed by front- and side-facing gables. The sand-colored, weathered-brick exterior conceals an innovative plan that begins with a recessed entry and portico, leading through the side courtyard to create an inviting processional to the formal entry. A secluded casita offers an easy transition from the front property to the patio and pool area, maintaining a vital link to the outdoors. The house is designed around the courtyard and covered patio, wrapping the edges of the outside living space with rows of French doors. Inside, perpendicular galleries take advantage of their ground-level orientation to capture natural light and views of the courtyard. During daylight hours, the shade offered by the covered patio adds a highly desired convenience, allowing casual meals and conversations to be enjoyed in a sheltered environment. On balmy evenings, the open courtyard inspires a deep appreciation of the dry desert climate.

About The Floor Plan: This C-shaped plan invites outdoor living, with a portico, courtyard and covered courtyard linking the home to the desert climate that surrounds it. The forward gallery opens to a formal dining room and, through a colonnade, to the family room, kitchen and nook. Oriented toward the rear perimeter and around the side/central courtyard, French doors increase light and circulation throughout the home's interior. Flexible spaces include an optional outdoor kitchen, which may be converted to guest quarters.

Legend

1 Entry Portal	9 Kitchen	17 Exercise Room
2 Casita	10 Nook	18 Bedroom Suite
3 Side Courtyard	11 Hall	19 Garage
4 Covered Courtyard	12 Powder Room	20 Bathroom
5 Entry	13 Laundry	21 Outdoor Kitchen
6 Gallery Hall	14 Retreat	22 Outdoor Dining
7 Dining Room	15 Master Bedroom	
8 Family Room	16 Master Bathroom	

3,490 SQUARE FEET

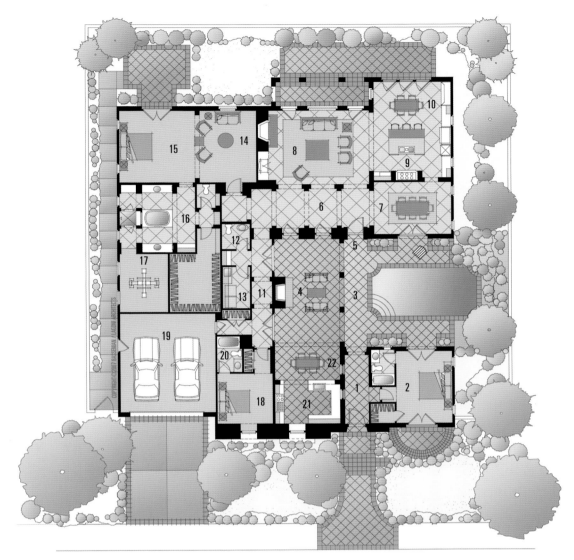

Right | Iron brackets and overhanging eaves affirm the Spanish roots of the design. Carriage lights flank a scrolled wrought-iron gate that leads through the portico to the courtyard.

Above | Cherry-colored cabinetry enriches a gourmet kitchen featuring a food-preparation island. The family room is arranged to allow family gatherings that include the cook.

Left | The side/central courtyard provides an idyllic outdoor environment for gatherings with guests or merely sunbathing. An arcade creates an airy border for the covered patio, and offers a unifying element for the arena. A detailed brick surround enriches the French doors leading to the casita.

Above | From the tiled entry hall, a series of arches telescopes toward the formal dining room, creating an impressive site line and airy boundary for the great room.

Below | A sculpted arch carved with a scalloped edge lends a subtle sense of separation to the master bedroom and the foreground sitting area, which features its own views of the back property.

Above | An outdoor fireplace with a masonry surround anchors the covered patio, and offers warmth and ambience to a generous, open-air sitting area overlooking the courtyard.

Destino at Vellano

BUILDER: SHEA HOMES • LOCATION: CHINO HILLS, CALIFORNIA • PHOTOGRAPHY: LANCE GORDON

THE COMMUNITY

Compatible arrangements of exterior styles organized on sloping lots create a village-like environment in this carefully planned neighborhood. Varying lot sizes honor the terrain, offering unique elevations at the streetscape. Authentic European themes employ stone, brick, tile and sunwashed hues to achieve harmony with the rural setting. Central courtyards create processional approaches to the formal entries of the homes. Arcaded galleries open the interiors to views and natural light, with key rooms positioned at the rear perimeters, where walls of glass and French doors connect the homes to their surroundings. Decks and covered patios enrich each plan's relationship to the outdoors.

Above Right | A central courtyard provides a generous outdoor living area with a fireplace and spatially connects the home and casita.

Right | A main-level master bedroom overlooks its hilly surroundings, and enjoys access to a covered patio shared with the breakfast room.

Below Right | In this single-level plan, a sculpted arch provides subtle definition to an open arrangement of the great room and kitchen.

The Cortile Collection at The Bridges

BUILDER: HCC INVESTORS/LENNAR COMMUNITIES • LOCATION: RANCHO SANTA FE, CALIFORNIA • PHOTOGRAPHY: ERIC FIGGE

RESIDENCE FOUR

Inspired by earlier renaissance styles, this formal Italian villa pairs a refined two-story stucco elevation with a square-pier entry. Flanked by a single-level wing, the forward vertical structure echoes the classic architectural proportions of a gentler era. Sited in a walkable community with an array of neighboring Tuscan-style estates, the home's grand symmetry conveys a street presence that is urban yet pedestrian-friendly, with the three-car garage placed at the side to preserve the vitality of the public view. As the plan unfolds, it is designed to allow spaces to take on a more relaxed scale, creating a balance that is straight-

forward yet stately. Beyond the front of this home, a side courtyard intentionally penetrates the footprint, increasing light and air at the core of the interior. The same attention to design is manifested around the elevation: at the rear perimeter, a protected loggia acts to soften the transition between the living area and the open back property. Designed to provide a sequential experience from the entry to the rear yard, the plan interposes a high-volume public zone with vistas and sightlines that extend toward the informal wing. The fluid progression of the home from the well-defined forward rooms to the open dimensions of the rear

Above | Panels of glass and French doors orient the casual living spaces at the back of the house toward views of the property and a sense of the outdoors. The earthy palette repeats the warm tones of Italian villas, while the wrought-iron balustrade is a characteristic elaboration of the style.

living spaces follows a design pattern prescribed for California, where a year-round climate calls for view-oriented informal zones. The spacious side courtyard, loggia, balcony and deck all enhance outdoor living experiences and invite an enjoyment of nature into the home. The plan integrates an elegant yet relaxed interior environment with convertible options that add flexibility: a main-level guest suite or home office, a walk-in entertainment bar or servery, and a secluded morning room that acts as an informal gathering area. Architectural details such as open beams, warm colors and simple square arches dominate the family room and kitchen. A book loft, which wraps the library, adds a sense of volume and space to the entire front of the home—another element of formality borrowed from centuries past.

About The Floor Plan: Formal rooms flank the entry of this well-scaled traditional plan. Under the library's 20-foot ceiling, an auxiliary staircase leads to an open book loft that adds a greater sense of space and light. Anchored by a central foyer, the gallery links the dining room with the courtyard via French doors, creating a connection with the outside space. A secluded master suite complements the upper-level sleeping quarters, and opens to a private deck.

Legend

1 Entry	9 Side Courtyard	17 Loggia
2 Living Room	10 Butler's Pantry	18 Garage
3 Music Room	11 Laundry	19 Book Loft
4 Powder Room	12 Wine Storage	20 Bedroom
5 Guest Bedroom	13 Walk-in Pantry	21 Master Bedroom
6 Bathroom	14 Morning Room	22 Master Bathroom
7 Dining Room	15 Kitchen	23 Deck/Balcony
8 Gallery Hall	16 Family Room	

5,234 SQUARE FEET

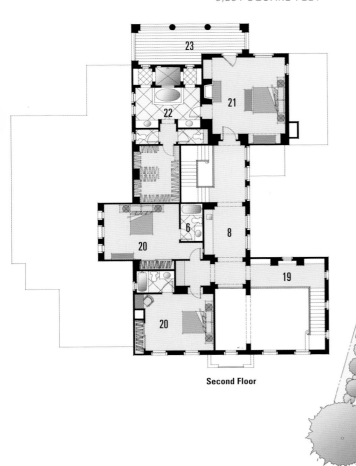

Second Floor

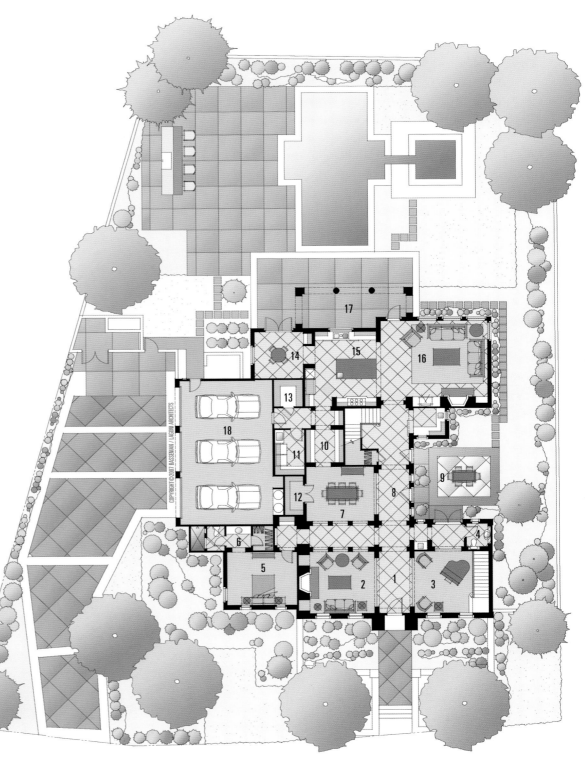

Opposite Page | Dual French doors open to the side courtyard, linking the alfresco living area to the formal dining room and to the stair hall, which adjoins a servery and wet bar. To the left, the space leads to the library and loft via a service hall.

Above | Framed by a colonnade of arches and anchored by a massive mantel and surround, the living room affirms the formality of the front of the plan. Rustic ceiling beams and glass-paneled cabinet doors give the room a desired connection to history.

Above | Paneled cream-colored cabinetry and pale leaf-green walls reinforce the soft interior motifs of the home in a kitchen designed for family gatherings as well as traditional occasions. The food-prep area adjoins a hall and butler's pantry that links to the formal dining room.

Elements of
Design

Classic Is Timeless

■ Pre-cast trim and corner elements drawn from an authentic European vocabulary contribute to this revival of Italian Renaissance style. Rows of pedimented windows flank the entry, suggesting a formality borrowed from later interpretations of the theme. Crafted brackets and detailed eaves dominate the cornice line beneath the low-pitched hipped roof, characteristic of Mediterranean design. Tonal variations in the stucco elevation enhance subtle changes of color and texture in the intentionally uneven rows of terracotta roof tiles. Significant embellishments, such as the Juliet balcony and wrought-iron balustrade above the entry, induce a pristine past with few concessions made to the passage of time. Shutters and surrounds on rows of windows replicate period features. Natural materials bestow a vintage character on the classic symmetry of the façade, which achieves visual fusion with the prevalent, more rustic, Tuscan architecture that shapes the community. True to the classic theme of the home, formal rooms are presented at the front of the floor plan, with the public areas open to the entry—an architectural element that has endured the test of time. Light is drawn into the house at the courtyard via the gallery, which serves as an axial element upstairs as well as downstairs, allowing myriad views of the outside space. Stacked architecture at the center and to the back of the plan also permits increased circulation and flow, and a sequential unfolding of the house on both levels.

542

The Lakes

BUILDER: LENNAR • LOCATION: RANCHO SANTA FE, CALIFORNIA
PHOTOGRAPHY: ERIC FIGGE

THE COMMUNITY

The Spanish colonial homes of The Lakes capture the spirit of Hollywood's Golden Era of architecture. Made popular by the works of such celebrated architects as George Washington Smith, Lilian Jenette Rice and Wallace Neff, these homes exhibit smooth, simple façades and balanced proportions that borrow heavily from Early California vernacular. The elevations employ a diverse range of forms, massing and heritage details to shape this community's rich street scene. Based on centuries-old Andalusian structures, the homes feature private courtyards that create harmony between interior spaces and the natural environment. Loggias, balconies and decks unite the rooms with their surroundings and effect sunny transitions to the enclosed gardens, courtyards and patios.

Above | Framed by a parabolic arch, the forecourt provides an inviting processional to the formal entry. A row of clerestory windows, underscored by a barrel-tile roof, helps define the forward loggia.

Opposite Page Above | A large, mullion window in the formal dining room brings in picturesque views of the San Dieguito River Valley. The archway to the rear of the room leads through a butler's pantry to the prep kitchen.

Opposite Page Center | With pure geometric forms, this Spanish Colonial Revival elevation creates an elegant composite of modern and heritage elements. A casita flanks the entry portico, topped by a deck and upper-level studio.

Opposite Page Below | A full complement of shed, hipped and cross-gabled rooflines defines this rear elevation, and authenticates the spirit of the plan. French doors line the loggia, and link the great room with views of the deck and pool.

Above | A graceful arcade and loggia add dimension to this rear elevation, which is further extended by a large patio with pool and decorative fountain. The asymmetry of the gables and stepped massing create natural rhythms that relate the house to its site.

Opposite Page Above | An informal arrangement of the great room and kitchen permits impromptu gatherings and conversation between guests and family. A simple square arch defines the separation between the food-preparation area and nook.

Opposite Page Below | Secluded to the side of the plan, the office is accessed from the entry foyer through an open archway. Windows allow abundant natural light to penetrate from the covered loggia and forecourt.

Wine Country Residence

AT PASO ROBLES

BUILDER: WOODY WOODRUFF CONSTRUCTION CO. • LOCATION: PASO ROBLES, CALIFORNIA • PHOTOGRAPHY: ERIC FIGGE

Quiet integrations of line and space play against the many moods of the sky in this modernist elevation, poised on the crest of a hill overlooking the coastal mountains of central California. Expressing native elements in a varied, intricate arrangement, the house retains a simple vocabulary of materials. Rugged fieldstone walls, heavy timber beams, and clay-tiled roofs replicate the rustic details of early pueblo dwellings, while parapets and a curved wall are converted to the bold, simple forms and intense colors of a contemporary exterior. Without front, side, or rear property-line constraints, the design rests organically on the hilltop, deploying crisp lines and smooth planes of color to effect unity with its surroundings. Broken into a collection of smaller buildings, the plan captures the simplicity of its setting with a series of geometric forms—rectangles and shed roofs—connected by a single curved axis. The approach to the entry is anchored by a sculpted terracotta-colored cylinder that offers contrast with the linear forms. Massive walls interlinked with small garden courtyards create transitions via sliding glass doors—portals that allow great fingers of light to penetrate the building forms. Oriented toward the sunset, the primary rooms step into the landscape and absorb views that on clear days extend for miles.

About The Floor Plan | A complex of buildings is linked by a curved axis that unifies the structure. Although the plan is not fully revealed at the entry, the entrance court immediately establishes a sense of logic, and the central gallery continues this organization from building to building through continual reference to the courtyards.

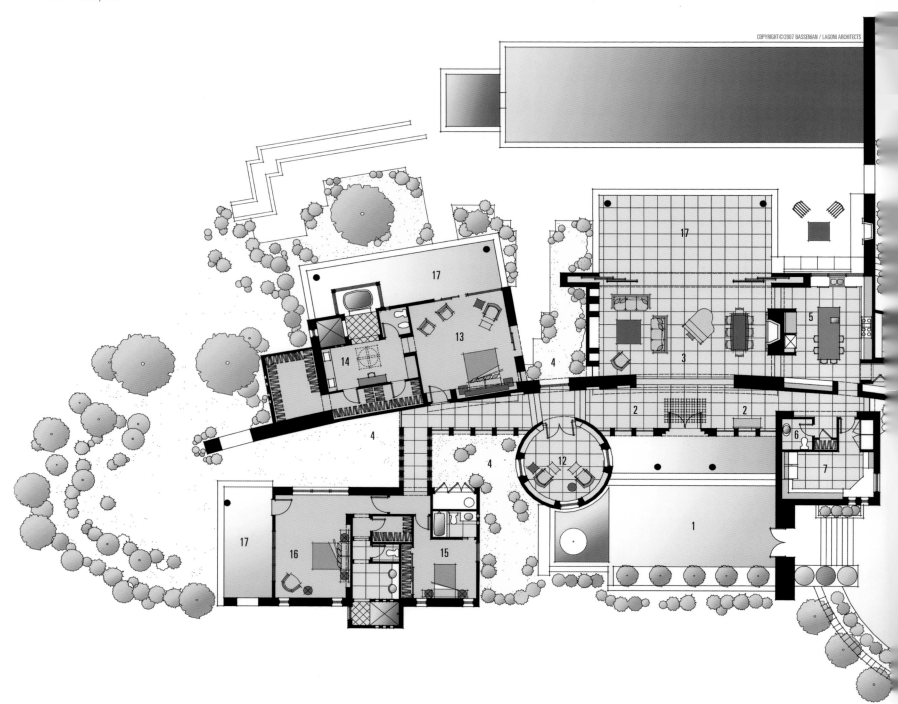

Previous Page | A stacked-fieldstone wall seems to rise from the rocky outcroppings that line the entry courtyard. House and garden are animated by brightly colored art balls—playful abstract sculptures designed to add scale and introduce whimsy at the point of arrival.

Right | Configured to capture the site's 360-degree views, the house is expressed in a series of primary forms, each building comprising one "hut" of the village-like cluster. A western orientation captures sunsets at the rear perimeter, and positions the home to overlook the owners' vineyards and a forest of oak groves.

Legend

1 Entry Courtyard	7 Laundry/Utility Room	13 Master Bedroom
2 Central Gallery Hall	8 Storage	14 Master Bathroom
3 Great Room	9 Mud Room	15 Bedroom
4 Courtyard	10 Pool Bathroom	16 Guest Suite
5 Kitchen	11 Garage	17 Covered Terrace
6 Powder Room	12 Library	18 Equipment Area

4,526 SQUARE FEET

Above | Receding glass doors offer a seamless integration with the outdoors between the indoor living area and the terrace. Bold forms create modern expressions that counter the warm textures of tile and wood.

Right | Concrete columns, steel beams and overhanging eaves define the boundaries of the sheltered outdoor living spaces. Multi-levels of Canterra stone allow ample spaces for open-air conversation groups, and create an engaging interplay with the rocky terrain.

Above | A triple-window view of the side property infuses the south-ern-most guest suite with a sense of nature. Wood ceiling panels conceal lighting fixtures that indirectly add a sense of warmth and vitality to the room.

Right | In the great room, views of the distant horizon mingle with elements of a modernist vocabulary. Pure shapes and sweeping lines unite the primary living space with an eloquent assemblage of light.

Above | Geometric forms pervade the primary rooms of the house, subdued by a mix of rustic and urbane materials. Raw timber beams contradict an intricate neon wall sculpture that adds splashes of sapphire, chartreuse and amethyst to the room's neutral palette.

Opposite Page | Harbored within the cylinder, the library offers a dramatic vista of the rolling hills to the east through a tall glass portal that blurs the boundary between indoors and out.

Above | Characterized by honest, unornamented materials, the master bedroom achieves integrity with its surroundings via glass portals that open to a garden courtyard.

Right | Beyond the cloud-white walls of the master bath, hilly stretches of oak groves and vineyards roll toward the coastal mountains—a view that becomes an integral part of the architecture and aesthetic of the home.

Above | The house is centered around the gallery, a curved axis which forms a passageway connecting the main living areas and organizing the flow and circulation of the home. Among the sculptures that line the hall, two wicker balls announce the entrance to the library.

Elements of
Design

Blending With The Environment

■ Like a village on the hilltop, the house responds to the site with a simple fusion of contrasting forms and minimalist details that engage the character of the rural surroundings. The individual qualities of each building are respected with organized rhythms of scenery that promote flow to the outside spaces. Spun with the basic architectural materials of steel, concrete, wood and plaster, the design conveys a sense of the outdoors through the use of stone and other natural elements on the inside. Bold forms that reach beyond the roofline are designed to create a dialogue between land and sky, and accentuate the exterior shapes. Garden spaces between the buildings are carefully located to permit daylight and glimpses of the view via glass window and door panels. Structural lines designed to obey the slope of the site create a contemporary framework for the strong colors and varied textures of wood and tile, softening the scale of the home. In a land of contrasts, the home exhibits versatility in its integrations of spatial, structural, and utility elements, and above all, its natural link to the surrounding environment.

Three-65 at Victoria Gardens

BUILDER: SHEA HOMES • LOCATION: RANCHO CUCAMONGA, CALIFORNIA • PHOTOGRAPHY: WILL HARE, JR.

An upscale collection of flats and townhomes, this neighborhood of attached residences represents a modern composite of Prairie architecture. Horizontal lines and low-pitched, hipped roofs typify the vernacular, adapted here to a compact urban scale suited to a mixed-use community. Layered surfaces and four-sided architecture create interest on the public and private sides of the buildings. Below the roof line, mullion patterns, which are inherent to Prairie and Bungalow styles, give emphasis to groupings of windows that dominate the elevations. Massive square piers that define outdoor living areas—a universal feature of this architecture—break the symmetry of the upper-level structures. Below the decks, large porches encased in red brick with arched, hearth-style openings symbolize the broad, flat chimneys of this vernacular. A third-story loft in one of four floor plans creates a tower room on one end of the building, adding asymmetrical elements to the roof planes.

Above | Interior windows lining an upper-level master suite overlook the living room. Light pours into the space through four clerestory windows, which add to the daylight brought in by a main-level picture window.

Above Right | In the kitchen, a peninsular counter doubles as a pass-through to a flexible space in the living area that has been converted to the dining room. The rectilinear pattern of the flooring echoes the horizontal bands and subtle dark-light geometry that typify the style.

Below Right | Vibrant combinations of brick, masonry and clapboard siding define the horizontal planes of the building. Wrought-iron rails and the use of brick and other materials lend a Prairie identity to the plan.

Altamura

BUILDER: WILLIAM LYON HOMES • LOCATION: LAGUNA HILLS, CALIFORNIA • PHOTOGRAPHY: ERIC FIGGE

RESIDENCE THREE

Nested high in the foothills at Nellie Gail Ranch, this clapboard-and-brick façade conceals an engaging 21st-century courtyard plan that adds light to the interior with an array of outdoor spaces. Dual porches, including one that wraps around a flexible home office or library, highlight the traditional East Coast exterior, which positions the swing garage away from the public view to create a pedestrian-friendly approach to the home. Designed to blend with the streetscape of the twenty-year-old neighborhood, this new home preserves the heritage of the region while integrating a modern, multi-function court to enhance the flexibility and flow of the plan. Inside, the entry foyer yields to a main gallery that permits access to both the covered and open areas of the central court, pro-viding an airy boundary for the dining room and stair hall. Traditional rooms are linked by the corridor, which floods the spaces with natural light from the court-yard via a series of French doors. Great views abide throughout the plan, and the home's relationship with the courtyard does more than expand the rooms. Designed to permit maximum light into the home, the perimeter edges forward and back, creating layers of spaces that transition from indoors to out. The living room employs tall windows to bring in a sense of the outdoors, and even the secluded library enjoys a connection to nature, wrapped by a spacious front porch. Upstairs, the master suite stretches across the width of the plan, provid-ing access to decks on both sides and permitting light to enter the home.

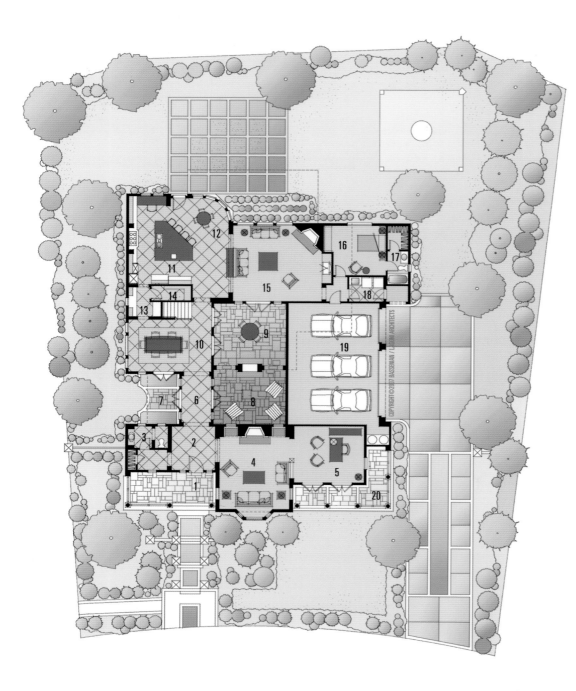

Second Floor

Legend

1 Entry Porch	10 Dining Room	19 Garage
2 Entry	11 Kitchen	20 Porch
3 Powder Room	12 Nook	21 Library/Loft
4 Living Room	13 Butler's Pantry	22 Master Bedroom
5 Home Office/Library	14 Walk-in Pantry	23 Master Bathroom
6 Gallery Hall	15 Family Room	24 Deck/Balcony
7 Side Courtyard	16 Bedroom	25 Game Room
8 Central Courtyard	17 Bathroom	
9 Covered Courtyard	18 Laundry	

5,776 SQUARE FEET

Opposite Page | Cloud-white clapboard siding sets off a central brick gable on a classic Northeastern elevation configured with broad outdoor spaces. An intimate sitting area softens the transition to the street and invites interactions with passers-by.

Previous Page | In the central courtyard, sculpted arches set in a brick wall frame a dual-sided fireplace, repeating the exterior materials of the home. A master deck overlooks the sitting area, while a covered patio behind the courtyard offers space for outdoor meals sheltered from the sun.

Foxfield

BUILDER: PARDEE HOMES • LOCATION: YORBA LINDA, CALIFORNIA • PHOTOGRAPHY: JEFF SMITH

RESIDENCE THREE

More cutting edge than convention, this courtyard home integrates a compelling mix of authentic materials with intuitive yet intellectual design. From the street, the home appears carved from the heart of Americana: a traditional exterior of classic clapboard siding—the color of fresh cream—enriched by a grey tile roof and a gable of decorative stone. Authentic details such as double-hung sashes, red-brick lintels and an upper-level balustrade reinforce the rural vocabulary, retuned to an appealing urban scale. The sheltered porch sets off a varied roofline that mimics the terraced terrain and helps to unite the plan with its hillside location. Inside, the plan offers a highly functional, 21st-century character with multiple living options and playful, unexpected spaces that heighten the versatility of the home. The side-court plan permits an exceptional degree of customization. Just off the entry, a bedroom suite converts to a home office, while the supersized family room may be split to incorporate a separate den or guest suite; upstairs, a wide loft might become Bedroom Five. An example of a well-organized home, the highly functional design offers a great sense of space, with intimate links to the outdoors. The open living and dining room arrangement grants a sweeping view of the central stairwell and loft, adding volume and dimension to the core of the home. French doors open the dining room to the side courtyard, a secluded, informal setting that supplements the large rear yard. Natural light is invited deep into the plan, permitting many opportunities for living out-of-doors.

Previous Page Above | The neat-as-a-pin traditional exterior is accentuated by white clapboard siding, decorative stone and grey roof tiles. A balcony from the upstairs family room adds detail to the front-facing gable over the garage.

Previous Page Below | A wide balcony accessible from the owners' suite overlooks a back property designed for outdoor living, while French doors and a trio of windows bring in natural light to the supersized family room. Both the strategically placed patio and spacious backyard, located conveniently off the casual zone, offer splendid areas for open-air meals and outdoor entertaining.

Above | Steps at the landing harbor a book loft brightened by a wide archway and views of the side property. Hardwood floors mingle with plush carpeting on the upper level, with the far wing designated as living and sleeping spaces for children.

Left | Contemporary colors play counterpoint to stained maple handrails and a hardwood floor in the public realm. The stairwell and loft present sweeping interior vistas above the formal dining room, enhanced by two-level volume and views to the side courtyard.

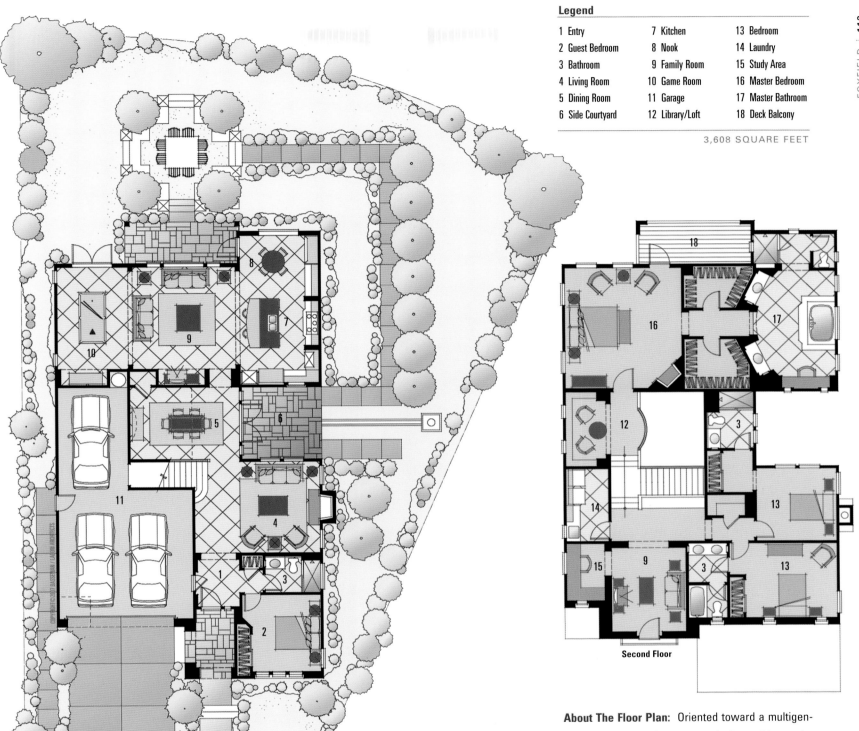

Legend

1 Entry	7 Kitchen	13 Bedroom
2 Guest Bedroom	8 Nook	14 Laundry
3 Bathroom	9 Family Room	15 Study Area
4 Living Room	10 Game Room	16 Master Bedroom
5 Dining Room	11 Garage	17 Master Bathroom
6 Side Courtyard	12 Library/Loft	18 Deck Balcony

3,608 SQUARE FEET

Second Floor

About The Floor Plan: Oriented toward a multigenerational market, the courtyard plan achieves the targeted size of nearly 4,000 square feet, set in an articulated footprint on an elevated site. Room options expand the function of both upper and lower levels, with a high bed and bath count, and alternatives that include such luxe amenities as a game room and book loft. Outdoor spaces are notched into the periphery to the side and rear of the plan, with a master deck above that overlooks the fairway.

Montanez at Covenant Hills

BUILDER: CENTEX HOMES • LOCATION: LADERA RANCH, CALIFORNIA • PHOTOGRAPHY: ANTHONY GOMEZ

RESIDENCE ONE

Set among the hills of San Juan Capistrano, this English Country elevation presents a series of prominent overlapping gables and steeply pitched rooflines, enriched by a rustic blend of brick and stucco. Varied eave lines, exposed rafter tails and recessed windows establish today's interpretation of a 19th-century Tudor-style cottage in an upscale community of eclectic styles. Versatile areas on the main floor include an airy, well-lit dining room that relates closely to the courtyard via a covered loggia. An adjoining butler's pantry, featuring an optional sink and wine cooler, leads to a dramatic space formed by an open arrangement of the morning room, kitchen and great room. A series of French doors along the rear perimeter brings in plenty of natural light and provides access to the back property, an inviting space that complements the function of the central court.

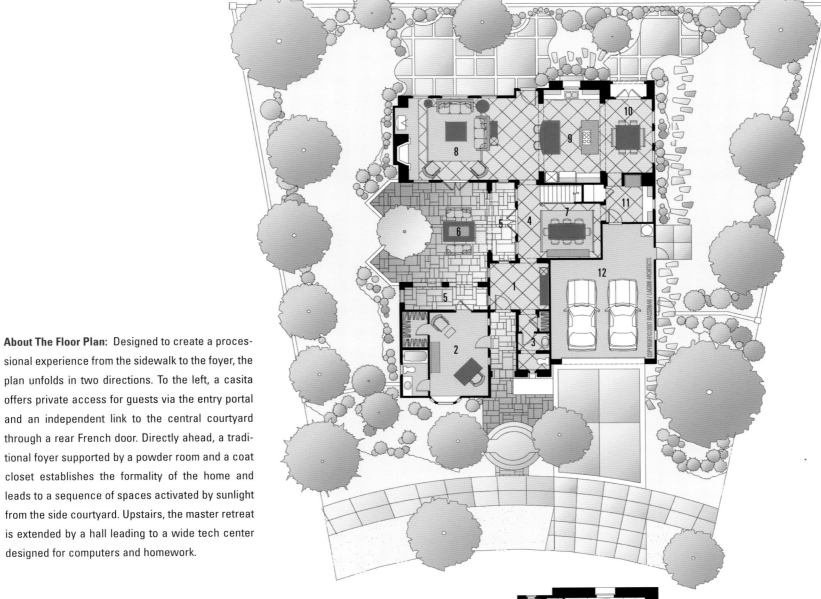

About The Floor Plan: Designed to create a processional experience from the sidewalk to the foyer, the plan unfolds in two directions. To the left, a casita offers private access for guests via the entry portal and an independent link to the central courtyard through a rear French door. Directly ahead, a traditional foyer supported by a powder room and a coat closet establishes the formality of the home and leads to a sequence of spaces activated by sunlight from the side courtyard. Upstairs, the master retreat is extended by a hall leading to a wide tech center designed for computers and homework.

Second Floor

Legend

1 Entry Foyer	8 Family Room	15 Study Area
2 Casita	9 Kitchen	16 Bedroom
3 Powder Room	10 Morning Room	17 Bathroom
4 Hall	11 Butler's Pantry	18 Master Bedroom
5 Covered Courtyard	12 Garage	19 Master Bathroom
6 Side Courtyard	13 Gallery Hall	
7 Dining Room	14 Laundry	

3,846 SQUARE FEET

Above | The formal dining room borrows light from the covered side courtyard, expanding the visual dimensions of the home without intruding on the tranquil facets of the outdoor space.

Above | A memorable kitchen results from the creation of dual islands: one designed to host informal meals and the other dedicated as a cook station. The space is intentionally scaled to foster intimate family gatherings yet boasts the capacity to serve a crowd.

Montanez at Covenant Hills

BUILDER: CENTEX HOMES • LOCATION: LADERA RANCH, CALIFORNIA • PHOTOGRAPHY: ANTHONY GOMEZ

RESIDENCE THREE

Infused with a sense of the outdoors, this courtyard home boasts wide views of the Capistrano hills and opens to a spacious courtyard at its core. Classical elements are present in the clean lines of the clapboard elevation: square columns and balustrades evoke the grace and beauty of Seaboard Colonial houses. Reflective of the geometry of seaside vernaculars, the pure forms of the entry portico capture the tranquility of a breezy waterfront cottage. From the street, a sense of informality reinforces the coastal origins of the plan. A three-car garage is set back from the street and intentionally de-emphasized, while a deep front porch offers outdoor living and friendship to its neighbors. Inside, a time-honored arrangement of the foyer and living room leads to a grand stair hall and a formal dining room with links to the courtyard. Adjacent to the casual living area, the courtyard serves multiple functions, not the least of which is to provide a splendid outdoor retreat.

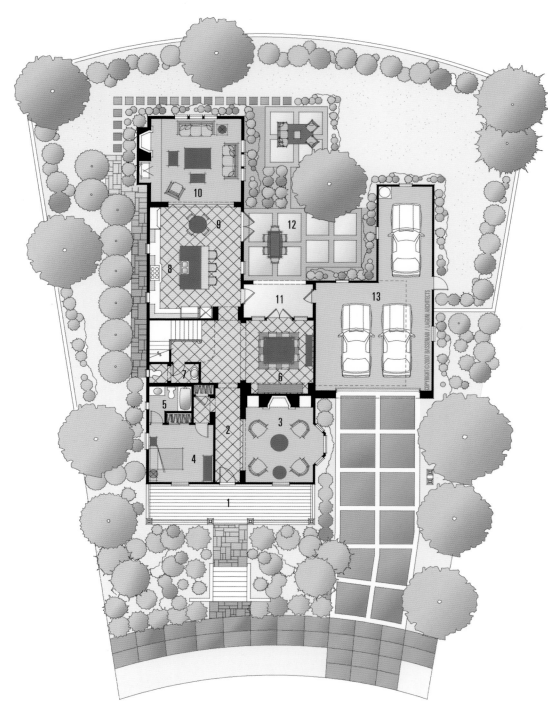

Second Floor

Legend

1 Entry Porch	8 Kitchen	15 Bedroom
2 Entry	9 Nook	16 Master Bedroom
3 Living Room	10 Family Room	17 Master Bathroom
4 Guest Bedroom	11 Covered Courtyard	18 Veranda
5 Bathroom	12 Rear Courtyard	19 Laundry
6 Dining Room	13 Garage	20 Deck/Balcony
7 Powder Room	14 Media Room	

3,730 SQUARE FEET

About The Floor Plan: Rooms positioned at the front of the plan exhibit the proportions necessary to achieve an eye-pleasing balance between the public and private sectors of the home. French doors connect the morning nook to the rear courtyard, while triple-window views of the space enrich the family room. Upstairs, a cluster of flexible spaces offers a series of links to the outdoors: a convertible bonus room provides access to a balcony linked to the master suite. Bedroom Two enjoys a private deck, while the larger bedroom suites share the veranda and views of the front property.

Previous Page | A sleek metal pavilion adds dimension and definition to the rear courtyard and harbors an intimate outdoor sitting area. Sight lines extend through an informal alfresco eating area and the covered courtyard to the formal dining room.

Opposite Page | An inviting extension of the upper floor plan, the veranda inspires fidelity to outdoor living, the enjoyment of fresh air and a love of the natural environment. A welcome counterpart to the central courtyard, this space offers a place of repose for the owners and their guests.

Above | Located to the rear of the plan, the family room extends the dramatic open space of the nook and kitchen. Surrounded by windows, the casual living area creates an airy retreat for guests and family, and links to the courtyard through the nook.

Above | Natural light filters through French doors from the courtyard to the morning nook and kitchen, illuminating cloud-white cabinetry and sleek 21st-century appliances, and amplifying the circulation of the private realm.

Front Street

BUILDER: STANDARD PACIFIC HOMES • LOCATION: LADERA RANCH, CALIFORNIA • PHOTOGRAPHY: LANCE GORDON

RESIDENCE TWO

One of California's most innovative neighborhoods, Front Street represents a practical alternative to suburban living, with a singular collection of live/work designs. A quadrant of 22 houses, the community is zoned for both commercial and residential use and presents a broad vocabulary of exterior styles that include Charleston-inspired Colonials, Monterey Haciendas and Nantucket Cape Cods. Wound with a network of pedestrian trails and paseos, the community effectively promotes a flourish of private businesses in an environment that also encourages bicycling, hiking and walking. Each plan accommodates a service-based commercial enterprise, with the placement of the work-at-home area to the front or rear, depending on the type of business. Professionals that require public interaction, such as an attorney or interior designer, benefit from a formal, street-facing entry; trades that focus on delivery-based services utilize the private loops and alleys that feed the alternate "front" doors. With the public's propensity to work at home, the project provides a ground-breaking view of live-work design, paving the way for the next great step in suburban evolution.

Elements of
Design

A Live/Work Concept

Above | Pre-wired for intelligent technology, the office space at the mezzanine (photo left) works as hard as the commercial area below (photo right). Upper-level views offer a corner-office ambience that enhances the private work area of the home.

Previous Page | A seamless approach to the outdoors is evident at the center of the plan, where a single French door expands the family's living space to a side courtyard. The loggia shelters the alfresco dining area from the sun, and leads into the work studio through a private side door.

Opposite Page Right | The rear alley entrance to the work space—the other "front door"—is as ordered and elegant as the formal streetside entrance to the home.

■ The aim: to create a house plus an office not a house that merely includes an office. The outcome: a home that delivers all of the desirable living spaces plus a private office with an effective commercial space that fits perfectly into its suburban surroundings. In refining and formalizing a practical and stylish live/work unit, necessary design distinctions emerged both in the plan forms and in the floor plan. Clearly distinguishing the residential entry to the home from the business entrance — while preserving a unified architectural character — dictated a seamless approach to the interior and outside living spaces. Creating a multi-level office space with a private-lane entrance to the rear of the plan segregates the business function and carries the Charleston-inspired, Plantation-style architecture around the home. Scaled columns, shuttered windows and clapboard siding evoke a 20th-century seaside manor, providing definition to the rear entrance. The design

Legend

1 Entry Porch	8 Office	15 Bedroom
2 Entry	9 Reception	16 Bathroom
3 Living Room	10 Garage	17 Laundry
4 Dining Room	11 Gallery Hall	18 Office/Loft
5 Kitchen	12 Master Bedroom	19 Side Courtyard
6 Family Room	13 Master Bathroom	
7 Powder Room	14 Deck/Balcony	

3,213 SQUARE FEET

Second Floor

Alley

Street

offers approximately 3,213 square feet, with nearly 700 square feet dedicated to the work area. Formal rooms placed to the front of the plan lead to an open arrangement of the family room and kitchen at the center, providing a transition to the work zone. Living areas are deftly connected to the whole house, with the work space/studio readily accessible from the residential zone yet not visible. Sightlines are broken by an L-shaped vestibule that subtly links to the business zone, ensuring a vital, intuitive separation of the office and family functions.

MiraBay

BUILDER: SABAL HOMES OF FLORIDA • LOCATION: APOLLO BEACH, FLORIDA • PHOTOGRAPHY: ROB/HARRIS PRODUCTIONS

TRADEWIND RESIDENCE

Tucked along the shores of an inlet of Tampa Bay, this Boca Grande home offers an excellent example of Old Florida architecture, capturing views of the water with an authentic coastal character. Horizontal wood siding, box-bay windows and a seamed metal roof are deftly crafted to showcase the authentic features of the home, a classic cross-gabled plan that strikes a balance between past and present. Highly visible from the waterside as well as the street, the elevation conveys the simple massing of the original style enlivened by an intricate notching of outdoor spaces into the front and rear of the footprint. A forecourt creates an inviting approach to a properly subdued entry; the opposing garages are turned in, away from the streetscene, to preserve the aesthetic of the public view. Along the rear perimeter, inside and outside living areas are oriented toward the waterfront—a screened lanai expands the dimensions of the core of the home and complements a starlight deck that opens the upper level to fresh air and views. The central volume contains the public spaces required for living and entertaining, framed by private sectors that lead outdoors. The master-down plan offers several convertible areas—such as the den and loft—as well as a series of playful elements, including a sunlit game room and a mid-level landing that eases the transition between the upper and lower floors.

Legend

1 Entry Porch	9 Family Room	17 Pool Bathroom
2 Entry	10 Walk-in Pantry	18 Gallery Hall
3 Living Room	11 Laundry	19 Bedroom
4 Dining Room	12 Master Bedroom	20 Bathroom
5 Lanai	13 Retreat	21 Game Room
6 Home Office	14 Master Bathroom	22 Deck/Balcony
7 Kitchen	15 Study	
8 Nook	16 Garage	

4,015 SQUARE FEET

About The Floor Plan: The straightforward H-shaped plan allows each area to open visually to the site yet permits privacy. From the foyer, a through-vista encompasses the central living and dining area, lanai and inlet. The informality of the plan is expressed by the open arrangement of rooms. Opposite the family room and kitchen, the master wing runs the full depth of the house and leads to the secondary garage, offering privacy for the owners. Upstairs, a wide loft overlooks the core living area and leads to a game room with access to the deck.

Above | A deeply set front porch runs the width of the elevation and establishes the informal tone of the house. Cloud-white Adirondack chairs inspire a sense of well-being in a setting of trim balustrades and robin's-egg-blue clapboard, wrested from the past.

Second Floor

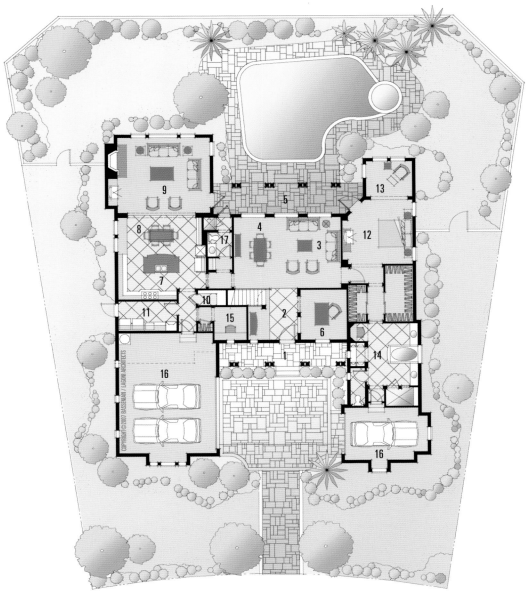

Above | Views of the bay and inlet invite repose in the owners' suite, which offers a private door to the pool and lanai. Just beyond the sleeping area, a sitting retreat defines the space with an intimate scale of its own.

Right | Oriented toward rear views, the private living and dining areas are infused with an inviting sense of informality that reinforces the seaboard character of the home. An open arrangement of the island kitchen, morning nook and family room allows for interaction between the work space and casual eating area, with plenty of places for people to gather.

Sutter's Mill

BUILDER: CENTEX HOMES • LOCATION: LADERA RANCH, CALIFORNIA • PHOTOGRAPHY: ERIC FIGGE

TOWNHOMES

Bold tones and cutting-edge lines create an award-winning tour de force in this urban-edge, high-density townhome community. Harbored by the hills of Terramor Village, Sutter's Mill reinforces the overall character of the surrounding area—a green-oriented neighborhood laced with foot trails and walkways—and connects with a network of arroyos, public courtyards and paseos that define the boundaries of the community. Fresh colors enliven elevations influenced by Bay Area row houses, Napa Valley farm buildings and historic mining structures from the Gold Rush era—revived here with striking dimensions and varied composi-

tions. Metal overhangs, cantilevered retreats and high-pitched rooflines integrate the contemporary character of the homes with the angled terrain. Carved into the setting with eco-friendly dimensions, each of the multi-plex clusters offers a quartet of distinctive plans, including a tri-level loft design. The structural purity and sustainability of each unit foster a heightened allegiance to the natural environment, a direction that has been well received by first-time buyers. A vital outcome of this approach was the community's immediate appeal to the intended market of professional singles, young couples and beginning families.

Above | An array of building forms reveals connectivity between the structures and their surroundings. The richly varied combination of textures and materials articulates the diversity of organic architecture.

Right | Colorful, upper-level retreats project above main-floor entries that address the sidewalk and connect each unit to the public realm.

Right | The turret harbors a loft retreat designed for the owners' repose. Layered massing and varied rooflines break up the scale and architectural components of the multi-plex clusters.

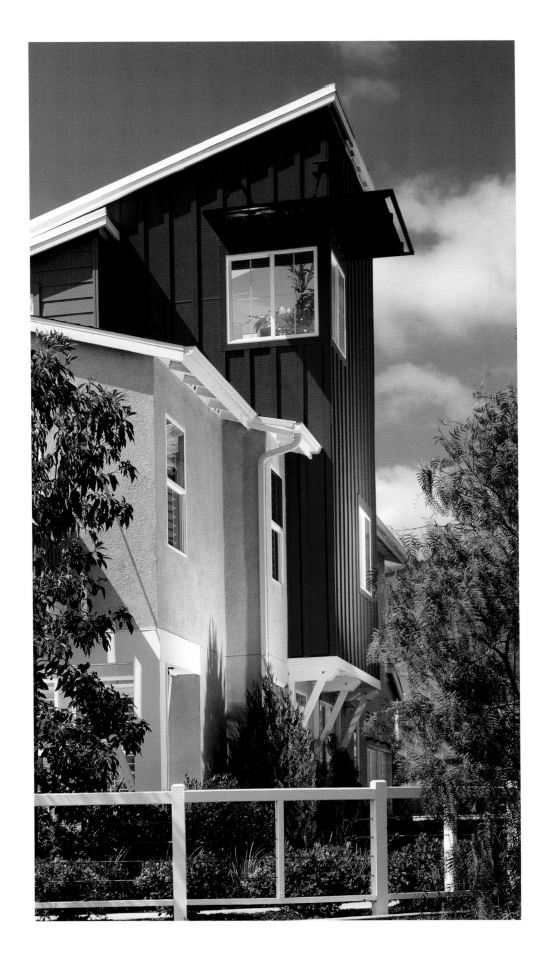

Opposite Page: A new concept in attached design, this high-density community features clusters of two- and three-level townhomes with pedestrian-friendly approaches and rear-loaded, direct-connect garages accessible via internal alleyways. Steeply angled rooflines and layered building forms create an informal aesthetic that is enriched with fresh combinations of lively colors. Materials such as steel-hung metal awnings and corrugated siding contrast with pure forms of wood and metal, and twist tradition toward an agrarian variation.

Elements of
Design

Fresh Colors & Eco-Sensitive Materials

■ A showcase of four-sided architecture, Sutter's Mill conveys a strong aesthetic by embracing the concept of livable, human-scaled design. Recognized with a national Best in American Living Award, a Gold Nugget for Best Attached Project, and numerous regional honors, the community is also known as a model for sustainable design. Within a green-oriented village, the homes provide a high level of energy-efficiency and sound ecological principles. Multi-layered elevations in vivid yet weathered tones mix stucco, wood and steel in innovative forms, obliques and perpendiculars, with strong lines that tower above surrounding rooftops. Branded "abstract national," the vernacular draws influence from iconic elements of farming and mining structures. Typical agrarian features, such as square turrets, balconies and steeply pitched gables, are reinvented by twisting traditional lines into a contemporized context. Corrugated siding and clapboard—time-honored

vestiges of rural vocabularies—are juxtaposed against high-profile gables and projecting forms, capturing an inventive character that recalls early California dialects. Combining vibrant architecture with a reverence for nature, the townhome community merges bold, contemporary design with eco-sensitive materials. Low-VOC paints and coatings, along with water-based finishes, integrate the splashy palette of hues with a dedication to environmentalism. Steel awnings, exposed beams and commercial cabling serve as counterpoints to raised-panel entry doors—a mere hint of the hand-troweled textures and crafted works inside. The unique mix of massing and materials distinguishes these townhouses from others in the master plan, creating a visually rich, ecologically responsible community.

CHAPTER TWO

ON THE BOARDS

Umm Al Quwain
Marina & Golf Resort

BUILDER: EMAAR • LOCATION: UNITED ARAB EMIRATES
WATERCOLOR RENDERINGS: MICHAEL ABBOTT

Scheduled for completion in 2011, this mixed-use development plan for a 1,500-acre site along the Arabian Gulf consists of a destination-resort marina town center, upscale golf course communities, a diverse mix of retail and entertainment facilities, and exclusive recreation areas. With an extensive marina at its core, the plan unfolds with clusters of villas and townhouses on manmade islands linked by navigable waterways. This self-sustaining development partners boutique hotels, waterfront resorts, shops, restaurants and commercial buildings with open beaches, piazzas, parks and hiking trails. The environment embodies a blend of historic and modernist vocabularies. Regular rhythms of surfaces, smooth and textured, paired with atriums and courtyards that emphasize circulation and privacy, counter classical elements with contemporary themes. A primary focus on scale and the careful placement of mixed-use buildings protects the live/work ethos, while natural materials, such as stucco and terracotta, create organic links with the setting.

Al Khobar Lakes Retail Center

BUILDER: EMAAR • LOCATION: SAUDI ARABIA

The Al Khobar Lakes Retail Center is part of a master-planned community located in Saudi Arabia near the Arabian Gulf. The Retail Center is strategically positioned adjacent to the intersection of two expressways, creating a community identity while at the same time establishing a destination point for the entire development. The intent of this localized amenity is to become the focal point for social, recreational, and leisure activities for the surrounding region. Visible from a great distance, the Al Khobar Retail Center has been integrated into the regional surroundings by providing a state-of-the-art facility complementing the local architectural character. The center is positioned to respond to the various climactic conditions of the region by supplying shaded areas, natural light to the interior, and operable fenestration for cross-ventilation. Acting as a terminus, the center evokes a strong sense of procession through dramatic entry features, hierarchical spaces, and rich interior textures and materials. The center will create a destination point for day-to-day activities, such as retail shopping, dining, health and day care, as well as areas for contemplation and retreat. The intent of the facility is to establish a location for neighborhood and local interaction and exchange.

NORTH ELEVATION

Mohali Hills

BUILDER: EMAAR/MGF • LOCATION: CHANDIGARH, INDIA
GRAPHICS: AMP 3D ZONE

Designed for upscale sectors of Chandigarh, a city defined a half-century earlier by LeCorbusier, this neighborhood of homes infuses India's roots with a current aesthetic. Scaled to a landmass of nearly 1,000 acres, clusters of villas and townhomes advance the area's residential ambience to a contemporary model of planned urbanism. Rigid geometry and palettes of neutral colors convey an aesthetic expressed by cubic forms and linear dimensions, with an emphasis on proportion, scale and detail. Single- and multi-family homes, interposed on compact lots, exhibit exteriors with smooth plaster-finished walls, pre-cast concrete coping and decorative parapet caps. Entries to individual homes are designed for maximum impact. Central and side courtyards offer outside living areas, while varied levels of rooftop terraces extend private retreats. Many homes, drawn to accommodate extended families, include thoughtfully positioned stairwells, which permit a conversion to separate living quarters at a future time.

20 50   100   200

0m

MOHALI HILLS

INSPIRED LIVING

Tinja

BUILDER: EMAAR/MOROCCO • LOCATION: TANGIER, MOROCCO • RENDERING: AMP 3D ZONE

TOWNHOMES

The architectural vernacular of the Tinja townhomes reflect a contemporary flavor with some influences from traditional motifs. The building cluster is a mixture of four attached homes — each celebrating outdoor living with courtyards, patios, balconies and roof terraces. Each home is designed with layered massing and composed to take full advantage of the nearby ocean and forest. The Tinja master-planned community is located in Tangier, an historic city in the north of Morocco that sits at the western tip of the Strait of Gibraltar where the Mediterranean Sea meets the Atlantic Ocean. This exceptional community fronts on the Atlantic Ocean on the west, a long stretch of native forest to the south and an ecologically rich river estuary to the north. At completion, the 730-acre (295-hectare) Tinja community will offer residents a vibrant town center with hotels, restaurants, a school, a beach club house, a sports facility and parks and lakes. Multiple residential offerings will include luxury villas, apartments (for-sale flats) and townhomes.

Luxury Villas
East OCT

BUILDER: OVERSEAS CHINA TOWN CO., LTD. • LOCATION: SHENZHEN, CHINA
GRAPHICS: ARCHIWOOD DESIGN DEVELOPMENT

A short drive from Shenzhen—China's center of foreign investment and one of the fastest growing cities in the world—this corporate retreat will offer repose for business executives in a secluded mountainside setting. Amid a landscape dotted with farms and lakes, the resort-style villa employs North American lodge architecture to deepen the rural character of a contemporary elevation that links closely with the outdoors. Hipped rooflines and overhanging eaves reinforce the clean simplicity of the façade's wide, horizontal layers, evoking elements of Prairie design. Decorative casement windows and sets of double French doors establish lines of symmetry supported by fieldstone and masonry piers. The plan comprises a network of rooms on four levels, which fully engage the site as the house progresses from one level to the next. Octagonal stairwells venture beyond the footprint, creating exterior paths between floors. The design reveals itself gradually, with elements of discovery planned for each space: a formal entry opens to a gallery that leads past a trio of formal spaces—a vaulted living room framed by a library and meeting room—toward a circular terminus and vectored wing that harbors the common areas, including a rustic dining hall.

Urban Infill Community

LOCATION: CALIFORNIA • RENDERING: MILO OLEA

MIXED-USE

A mixed-use development, this plaza provides a retail center at ground level and spacious residential flats throughout the upper floors. With a unique corner identity, the contemporary structure energizes the street with a lively palette of colors and sculpted forms. The forward-thinking residences include such features as two master suites and private balconies.

Annotated Projects List

Altamura
Residence Three
Laguna Hills, California
2003
Pages 106-109

Bassenian/Lagoni Architects Team:
Designers: Dave Pockett,
  Mike Pilarski
Project Managers: Sophia Braverman,
  John Oravetz

Builder: William Lyon Homes
Builder Executive in Charge of Design:
  Tom Mitchell
Landscape Architect: Urban Arena
Interior Designer: Design Tec Interiors
Structural Engineer: Performance Plus
  Engineering

Photographer: Eric Figge

Awards:
Best in American Living Awards 2004
  Home of the Year
National Sales & Marketing Awards 2004
  Silver Award
Gold Nugget Awards 2004
  Grand Award
MAME Awards/Southern California 2003
  Finalist

Bella Fioré at Lake Las Vegas
The Community
Henderson, Nevada
2006
Pages 26-31

Bassenian/Lagoni Architects Team:
Designers: Hans Anderle, Jeff Lake AIA
Project Manager: Luis Chavez

Builder: Pardee Homes
Builder Executives in Charge of Design:
  Bob Clauser, Loren Smets
Landscape Architect: SJA
Interior Designer: Color Design Art
Structural Engineer: Borm Associates

Photographer: Eric Figge

Awards:
Gold Nuggets 2006
  Merit Award
National Sales and Marketing Awards
  Silver Award

Casa Bonita del Rio
Rancho Santa Fe, California
2006
Pages 48-51

Bassenian/Lagoni Architects Team:
Designer: Joe Abrajano
Project Manager: Mike Pilarski

Client: Lance and Anna Waite
Landscape Architect: Gillespie Moody
  Patterson
Interior Designer: Design Visions
Structural Engineer: Performance Plus

Photographer: Eric Figge

Awards:
Gold Nugget Awards 2007
  Merit Award

Castellina at Covenant Hills
Ladera Ranch, California
2005
Pages 56-63

Bassenian/Lagoni Architects Team:
Designers: Dave Kosco AIA,
  Joe Abrajano, Raffi Agaian
Project Managers: Jeff Ganyo,
  Ian Sparks

Builder: Centex Homes – Southern
  California Coastal Division
Builder Executives in Charge of Design:
  Richard Douglass, Nick Lehnert
Landscape Architect: Borthwick Guy
  Bettenhausen
Interior Designer: Design Tec Interiors
Structural Engineer: Van Dorpe Chou
  Associates

Photographer: Eric Figge

Awards:
Best in American Living Awards 2005
  Residence 4 – Silver Award
National Sales & Marketing Awards 2005
  Residence 4 – Silver Award
Gold Nuggets 2005
  Attached Project – Merit Award
Gold Nuggets 2006
  Community Site Plan – Merit Award
  Attached Neighborhood – Merit Award
  Community of the year – Merit Award
MAME Awards/Southern California 2004
  Attached Community of the Year
    Winner

**The Cortile Collection
at The Bridges**
Residence Four
Rancho Santa Fe, California
2004
Pages 76-83

Bassenian/Lagoni Architects Team:
Designers: Dave Kosco AIA,
 Craig Gambill AIA
Project Manager: Brian Neves AIA

Builder: HCC Investors/Lennar
 Communities
Builder Executive in Charge of Design:
 Tom Martin
Landscape Architect: Pinnacle Design
Interior Designer: Pacific Dimensions
Structural Engineer: Performance Plus
 Engineering

Photographer: Eric Figge

Awards:
Gold Nuggets 2004
 Project of the Year – Grand Award
Gold Nuggets 2006
 Merit Award
MAME Awards/Southern California 2006
 Finalist
SAM Awards 2006 – Winner

Destino at Vellano
The Community
Chino Hills, California
2006
Pages 74-75

Bassenian/Lagoni Architects Team:
Designers: Dave Kosco AIA, Ryan White
Project Manager: Jeff Marcotte

Builder: Shea Homes
Builder Executive in Charge of Design:
 Bob Yoder
Landscape Architect: Forma Design
Interior Designer: Oma Talley Design
Structural Engineer: ESI/FME

Photographer: Lance Gordon

Awards:
Laurel Awards 2006
 Best Community – Winner
 Residence 2 – Winner
 Residences 1, 3 and 4 – Finalists

Foxfield
Residence Three
Yorba Linda, California
2005
Pages 110-113

Bassenian/Lagoni Architects Team:
Designers: John Bigot AIA, Jeff Lake AIA
Project Manager: Ian Sparks

Builder: Pardee Homes
Builder Executive in Charge of Design:
 Bob Clauser
Landscape Architect: SJA
Interior Designer: Color Design Art
Structural Engineer: Gouvis Engineering

Photographer: Jeff Smith

Awards:
ELAN Awards 2005
 Detached Community of the Year
 Finalist

Front Street
Residence Two
Ladera Ranch, California
2003
Pages 124-127

Bassenian/Lagoni Architects Team:
Designers: Dave Kosco AIA,
 Craig Gambill AIA
Project Manager: Ken Niemerski AIA

Builder: Standard Pacific Homes
Builder Executives in Charge of Design:
 Todd Palmaer, Ralph Spargo
Landscape Architect: Summers/Murphy
 & Partners
Interior Designer: Design Tec Interiors
Structural Engineer: Structural Design
 Group

Photographer: Lance Gordon

Awards:
Best in American Living Awards 2003
 Best Community – Platinum Award
 Residence 2 – Gold Award
National Sales & Marketing Awards 2003
 Residence 2 – Silver & Regional Awards
Gold Nuggets 2003
 Site Plan – Grand Award
 Residence 2 – Grand Award
MAME Awards/Southern California 2003
 Winner

Magazine Cover: Builder Magazine,
 September 2003

The Lakes
The Community
Rancho Santa Fe, California
2007
Pages 84-89

Bassenian/Lagoni Architects Team
Claybourne Product
 Designer: Joe Abrajano
 Project Managers: Jeff Ganyo,
  Brian Neves AIA, Sophia Braverman,
  Derek Sabor
Edgewater Product
 Designers: Craig Gambill AIA,
  Raffi Agaian, Ryan Sullivan
 Project Manager: Marty Lopez

Builder: Lennar
Builder Executives in Charge of Design:
 Mike Levesque, Tom Martin
Landscape Architect: Pinnacle Design
Interior Designer: Pacific Dimensions
Structural Engineer: Swanson &
 Associates

Photographer: Eric Figge

Awards:
Sam Awards 2007 – Winner
 Residence 2

MiraBay
Tradewind Residence
Apollo Beach, Florida
2005
Pages 128-131

Bassenian/Lagoni Architects Team:
Designers: Hans Anderle, Jason Yaw
Project Manager: Mike Beam

Builder: Sabal Homes of Florida
Builder Executive in Charge of Design:
 Bill Lee
Landscape Architect: Dunlap &
 Associates
Interior Designer: Creative Design
 Consultants
Structural Engineer: Silcox, Kidwell &
 Associates

Photographer: Rob/Harris Productions

Awards:
National Sales & Marketing Awards 2005
 Gold & Regional Winner
Aurora Awards 2005
 Best Detached Single Family Home
 Best Kitchen
 Best Interior Detailing
 Best Master Bath
Tampa Bay Parade of Homes 2006
 Grand Award
Tampa Bay Parade of Homes 2007
 Grand Award
MiraBay Newland Communities 2006
 Outstanding Architecture
  Grand Award

Magazine Cover: Professional Builder,
 May 2005

Montanez at Covenant Hills
Residence One
Ladera Ranch, California
2005
Pages 114-117

Bassenian/Lagoni Architects Team:
Designers: Dave Kosco AIA,
 Joe Abrajano, Raffi Agaian
Project Managers: Jeff Ganyo,
 Sophia Braverman

Builder: Centex Homes – Southern
 California Coastal Division
Builder Executives in Charge of Design:
 Richard Douglass, Nick Lehnert,
 Rick Wood
Landscape Architect: Borthwick Guy
 Bettenhausen
Interior Designer: Studio Design Group
Structural Engineer: Van Dorpe Chou
 Associates

Photographer: Anthony Gomez

Awards:
MAME Awards/Southern California 2005
 Best Detached Community – Finalist
 Residence 1 – Winner

Montanez at Covenant Hills
Residence Three
Ladera Ranch, California
2005
Pages 118-123

Bassenian/Lagoni Architects Team:
Designers: Dave Kosco AIA,
 Joe Abrajano, Raffi Agaian
Project Managers: Jeff Ganyo,
 Sophia Braverman

Builder: Centex Homes – Southern
 California Coastal Division
Builder Executives in Charge of Design:
 Richard Douglass, Nick Lehnert,
 Rick Wood
Landscape Architect: Borthwick Guy
 Bettenhausen
Interior Designer: Studio Design Group
Structural Engineer: Van Dorpe Chou
 Associates

Photographer: Anthony Gomez

Awards:
Gold Nugget Awards 2006
 Merit Award
MAME Awards/Southern California 2005
 Best Detached Community – Finalist

The Province
Residence Four
Indian Wells, California
2007
Pages 64-67

Bassenian/Lagoni Architects Team:
Designers: Raffi Agaian, Alan Nguyen
Project Manager: Sophia Braverman

Builder: Standard Pacific Homes
Builder Executives in Charge of Design:
Ram Fullen, Gary Carlson
Landscape Architect: HRP Studio
Interior Designer: Meridian Interiors
Structural Engineer: Structures Design
Group

Photographer: Anthony Gomez

Awards:
Gold Nuggets 2007
Merit Award

The Province
Residence Five
Indian Wells, California
2007
Pages 68-73

Bassenian/Lagoni Architects Team:
Designers: Raffi Agaian, Alan Nguyen
Project Manager: Sophia Braverman

Builder: Standard Pacific Homes
Builder Executives in Charge of Design:
Ram Fullen, Gary Carlson
Landscape Architect: HRP Studio
Interior Designer: Meridian Interiors
Structural Engineer: Structures Design
Group

Photographer: Anthony Gomez

Awards:
Gold Nuggets 2007
Merit Award

Rimrock Summit
The Community
Hidden Meadows, California
2006/2007
Pages 52-55

Bassenian/Lagoni Architects Team:
Designers: Ray Hart, Stacie Arrigo
Project Managers: Jeff Ganyo,
Mike Beam, Marty Lopez

Builder: Mastercraft Homes
Builder Executives in Charge of Design:
Daniel Thompson, Bob Liewer
Landscape Architect: Land Concern
Interior Designer: Blackbird Interiors
Structural Engineer: Gouvis Engineering

Photographer: Lance Gordon

Awards:
Gold Nuggets 2007
Detached Community – Merit Award
Residence 1 – Merit Award

Shady Canyon Residence
Irvine, California
2006
Pages 32-43

Bassenian/Lagoni Architects Team:
Designer: Joe Abrajano
Project Manager: Jeff Marcotte

Client: Jeff Roos
Landscape Architect: Katzmaier Newell
Kehr
Interior Designers: Dana Blower Design,
Christopher Kinne
Structural Engineer: Gouvis Engineering

Photographer: Eric Figge

Sutter's Mill
Ladera Ranch, California
2004
Pages 132-137

Bassenian/Lagoni Architects Team:
Designers: Dave Kosco AIA,
   Steven Dewan AIA, John Bigot AIA
Project Managers: Jeff Ganyo,
   Ian Sparks

Builder: Centex Homes – Southern
California Coastal Division
Builder Executives in Charge of Design:
   Richard Douglass, Nick Lehnert
Landscape Architect: Borthwick Guy
   Bettenhausen
Interior Designer: Rooms Interiors
Structural Engineer: Van Dorpe Chou
   Associates

Photographer: Eric Figge

Awards:
Best in American Living Awards 2004
   Best Attached Project – Platinum Award
National Sales & Marketing Awards 2004
   Residence 4 – Gold and Regional Awards
Gold Nugget Awards 2005
   Attached Project – Grand Award
   Attached Project of the Year –
      Merit Award
Gold Nugget Awards 2004
   Best Attached Project – Merit Award
American Institute of Architects/Orange
County 2004
   Honor Winner
MAME/Southern California 2004
   Attached Project – Finalist

Magazine Cover:
Professional Builder, November 2004

Three-65 at Victoria Gardens
Rancho Cucamonga, California
2007
Pages 104-105

Bassenian/Lagoni Architects Team:
Designers: Dave Kosco AIA, Raffi Agaian
Project Manager: Scott Bunney

Builder: Shea Homes
Builder Executive in Charge of Design:
   Bob Yoder
Landscape Architect: The Collaborative
   West
Interior Designer: Garrett Interiors
Structural Engineer: ESI/FME

Photographer: Will Hare, Jr.

Awards:
Gold Nugget Awards 2007
   Attached Project – Merit Award
   Attached Project of the Year –
      Merit Award
Builders Choice 2007
   Grand Award Winner
Best in American Living Awards 2007
   Best Single Family Attached –
      Platinum Award

The Tides at Crystal Cove
Residence One
Newport Coast, California
2007
Pages 14-25

Bassenian/Lagoni Architects Team:
Designers: Dave Kosco AIA,
   Joe Abrajano,
Project Manager: Brian Neves AIA

Builder: Standard Pacific Homes –
   Gallery Communities
Builder Executives in Charge of Design:
   Todd Palmaer, Ralph Spargo
Landscape Architect: Summers/Murphy
   & Partners
Interior Designer: Pacific Dimensions
Structural Engineer: Structures Design
   Group

Photographer: Anthony Gomez

Awards:
National Sales & Marketing Awards 2007
   Residence 1 – Silver Award

Tremezzo at Lake Las Vegas
Residence Two
Henderson, Nevada
2007
Pages 44-47

Bassenian/Lagoni Architects Team:
Designers: Hans Anderle, Jeff Lake AIA,
   Stacie Arrigo, Will Francisco
Project Manager: Brian Cameron

Builder: Pardee Homes
Builder Executives in Charge of Design:
   Bob Clauser, Loren Smets
Landscape Architect: SJA
Interior Designer: Color Design Art
Structural Engineer: Borm Associates

Photographer: Eric Figge

Awards:
National Sales & Marketing Awards 2007
   Residence 2 – Silver Award

Wine Country Residence
Paso Robles, California
2006
Pages 90-103

Bassenian/Lagoni Architects Team:
Designers: Steven Dewan AIA,
   John Bigot AIA
Project Manager: Mike Beam

Builder: Woody Woodruff Construction
   Company
Landscape Architect: Land Concern
Interior Designer: Marilyn Riding Design
Construction Documents: Randall Barnett
Structural Engineer: Jeffrey Schneidereit
   Architects
Lighting Consultant: Linda Ferry Lighting
   Design

Photographer: Eric Figge

Awards:
Gold Nugget Awards 2007
   Merit Award
MAME Awards/Southern California 2007
   Best Custom Home – Winner
Best in American Living Awards 2007
   Best One-of-a-Kind Custom Home
   Gold and Regional Winner
National Sales & Marketing Awards 2007
   Best One-of-a-Kind Home 2007
   Gold and Regional Award

Al Khobar Lakes
Retail Center
Saudi Arabia
2007
Pages 142-143

Bassenian/Lagoni Architects Team:
Designer: Ali Badie AIA

Builder: Emaar
Builder Executives in Charge of Design:
 Mark Amirault, Nasreldain Mahamoud

Luxury Villas
East OCT
Shenzhen, China
2007
Pages 148-149

Bassenian/Lagoni Architects Team:
Designer: Wenfei Feng

Builder: Overseas China Town Co., Ltd.
Builder Executives in Charge of Design:
 Jian Dian, Judy Qiao

Graphics: Archiwood Design
 Development

Mohali Hills
Villa Homes
Chandigarh, India
2007
Pages 144-145

Bassenian/Lagoni Architects Team:
Designers: Albern Yolo, Robert Orosa AIA

Builder: Emaar/MGF
Builder Executive in Charge of Design:
 Scott Pottruff

Rendering: AMP 3D Zone

Tinja
The Townhomes
Tangier, Morocco
2007
Pages 146-147

Bassenian/Lagoni Architects Team:
Designers: Ali Badie AIA, Romeo Ty

Builder: Emaar/Morocco
Builder Executives in Charge of Design:
 Wafaa Snibla
 Turner International

Rendering: Romeo Ty

Umm Al Quwain
Marina & Golf Resort
United Arab Emirates
2006
Pages 140-141

Bassenian/Lagoni Architects Team:
Designer: Ali Badie AIA

Builder: Emaar
Builder Executives in Charge of Design:
 Scott Pottruff, Sana Farooq

Rendering: Michael Abbott

Urban Infill Community
California
2006
Pages 150-151

Bassenian/Lagoni Architects Team:
Designers: Ali Badie AIA,
 Paul Fulbright AIA

Rendering: Milo Olea

Staff List 2007

Executive Staff
Aram Bassenian
Carl Lagoni
Scott Adams
Ali Badie
Steven Dewan
Dave Kosco
Jeff LaFetra
Jeff Lake
Ken Niemerski
Lee Rogaliner

Vice Presidents
Mike Beam
Robert Chavez
Ernie Gorrill
Nick Lehnert
Brian Neves
Dave Pockett

Vice President, China Operations
Yao Wang

Director of Marketing
Heather McCune

Associate Vice Presidents
Hans Anderle
Craig Gambill
Jeff Ganyo
Marty Lopez
Edie Motoyama
Robert Orosa

Senior Associates
John Bigot
Sophia Braverman
Ray Hart
Jeff Marcotte

Associates
Kevin Burt
Brian Cameron
Dave Day
Judy Forrester
George Handy
Curtis Ong
Tony Vinh
Wendy Woolsey

General Staff
Joe Abrajano
Raffi Agaian
Stacie Arrigo
Edwin Balquiedra
Jesse Barrera
Rafael Bello
Karen Bestone
Bruce Bishara
Randy Brown
Scott Bunney
Dwayne Butz
Eva Caranay
Lenz Casilan
Sergio Cecena
Luis Chavez
Johnny Chung
Freddy Conrado
Sue Dewan
Jenni Dillon
Kele Dooley
Dee Drylie
Maleck Elahi
Ginger Elkins
Gerry Encarnacion
Alicia Erickson
Todd Evans
Jorge Favila
Joey Feld
Wenfei Feng
Jornell Franciliso
Will Francisco
Paul Fulbright
Casey Galyean
Mike Gilbert
Kevin Groves
Joohyun Her
Young Hong
Roberta Jeannette
Alison Jones
Joel Jose
Erik Kelenc
James Kim
Alan Knebel
John Kounlavong
Huy Le
Mark Leasor
Jason Lee
Ji Sun Lee
Phillip Lee
David McClean
Kristina McVeigh
Jose Mendez

Carlos Meneses
Laura Minott
Tom Mkhitaryan
Christina Nagel
Alan Nguyen
Ronnie Ojeda
Jacob Olid
John Oravetz
Carlos Pelayo
Margo Penick
Jeremy Phillips
Mike Pilarski
Susan Pistacchi
Rachel Pockett
Gregory Purvis
Tarane Rahmani
Yvonne Ramos
Rod Reyes
Jeff Roach
Nate Rodholm
Ryan Rosecrans
Erin Ryan
Derek Sabor
Katya Sato
Selma Saxton
Jesika Scherzinger
Anna Shakun
Andrew Silder
Jeffry Sinarjo
Debora Smith
Tracy Smith
Ian Sparks
Dawn Stanton
Michael Stone
Kevin Stracner
Ellen Sung
Janet Thomas
Romeo Ty
Chris Velasquez
Linda Velasquez
April Villa
Long Vu
Warren Walker
Jill Warren
James West-Herr
Ryan White
Eric Widmer
John Wilmert
Michael Wu
Wenling Wu
Albern Yolo
Bernard Yuen

Index